MW01298065

D Day
A Captivating Guide to the Battle for Normandy

Created by

Captivating History

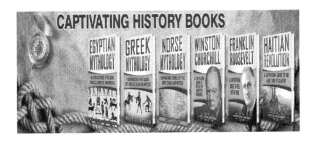

© Copyright 2017

All rights Reserved. No part of this book may be reproduced in any form without permission in writing from the author. Reviewers may quote brief passages in reviews.

Disclaimer: No part of this publication may be reproduced or transmitted in any form or by any means, mechanical or electronic, including photocopying or recording, or by any information storage and retrieval system, or transmitted by email without permission in writing from the publisher.

While all attempts have been made to verify the information provided in this publication, neither the author nor the publisher assumes any responsibility for errors, omissions, or contrary interpretations of the subject matter herein.

This book is for entertainment purposes only. The views expressed are those of the author alone, and should not be taken as expert instruction or commands. The reader is responsible for his or her own actions.

Adherence to all applicable laws and regulations, including international, federal, state, and local laws governing professional licensing, business practices, advertising, and all other aspects of doing business in the US, Canada, UK, or any other authority is the sole responsibility of the purchaser or reader.

Neither the author nor the publisher assumes any responsibility or liability whatsoever on the behalf of the purchaser or reader of these materials. Any perceived slight of any individual or organization is purely unintentional.

Contents

Free Bonus from Captivating History (Available for a Limited time)

Hi History Lovers!

Now you have a chance to join our exclusive history list so you can get your first history ebook for free as well as discounts and a potential to get more history books for free! Simply visit the link below to join.

Captivatinghistory.com/ebook

Also, make sure to follow us on:

Twitter: @Captivhistory

Facebook: Captivating History: @captivatinghistory

Introduction

D-Day, the Allied invasion of German-held Normandy, was one of the most extraordinary achievements not only of the Second World War but in the whole of military history. Millions of Allied personnel were involved in launching the greatest sea-borne invasion ever undertaken. Incredible acts of cunning and of courage ensured success in an operation that changed the face of the war, opening a vast new front. It led to the liberation of France and the defeat of Nazi Germany.

Why was this extraordinary operation launched? How was it done? And what happened in the aftermath?

Chapter 1 – Why D-Day?

The Second World War was a conflict unlike any other that had come before. During the First World War, a network of alliances had turned a war in the Balkans into one that engulfed all of Europe, but fighting in the rest of the world was limited. World War Two, on the other hand, brought together a long-standing war between Japan and China, German attempts to create a European empire, and battles for control of colonies across Africa and Asia. When Japanese ambitions brought America into the fighting in 1941, it became a single maelstrom of destruction that spanned the globe, involving every leading military power and dozens of other nations.

In Europe, the Axis powers of Germany and Italy were the aggressors at every turn. The Germans occupied vast swathes of eastern Europe, half of Scandinavia, and western Europe all the way to the Atlantic Ocean. The fall of France briefly left Britain as the only sovereign and unconquered nation in Europe still opposing this tide of blood. The British, aided by their colonies, allies in the Commonwealth, and thousands of soldiers who had fled the conquered countries, fought on in the skies above Europe and in colonial possessions around the world, especially North Africa, where fighting swayed back and forth from early in the war.

It was the arrival of the Americans that turned the tide of that campaign. Though it was a Japanese attack that brought them into the war, from the start, they made Europe their main priority. They believed it would be easier to defeat Germany first and then its ally Japan.

The Americans joined the British in North Africa late in 1942, bringing their substantial economic resources and a vast pool of manpower to bear. Though the campaign had its setbacks, it signaled the near-inevitable defeat of the Axis powers in the face of superior resources. The Allies drove the Axis forces back into a smaller and smaller pocket in north-east Tunisia until the last Germans and Italians were forced to surrender.

North Africa was important for the control of supply routes, but it was also a springboard for an invasion of Europe. Behind the scenes, the British and Americans continued to argue about how to knock out Germany, the leader of their European opponents and the most powerful enemy in that theatre of the war. The Americans favored developing a grand plan to invade France, liberating another potentially powerful ally, and push from there directly into Germany. The British, who had fewer resources and struggled from the start with the strength of the German military, favored a more cautious approach, fighting step-by-step, taking opportunities as they came. If they could win the war by bombing Germany or invading through some other route, they could avoid the costs and risks of a sea-borne landing in France.

The result was a compromise. Some resources were put into invading Italy from Africa in 1943, while a larger portion were held in reserve to invade France the following year.

The Italian campaign was a success, as that country's government almost immediately flipped sides, forcing the Germans and those Italians who backed them to fight against local resistance as well as foreign invaders. But it was a slow-burning campaign in which Kesselring, the German commander, built a series of defensive lines that slowed down and eventually halted the Allied advance.

Meanwhile, the war was turning against the Germans in Eastern Europe. Having betrayed and invaded their former allies in the Soviet

Union, the Germans became bogged down in a grueling war against a nation of immense resources and unquenchable determination. The Eastern Front became a huge drain on the German war machine, making a successful invasion in the west more plausible.

Russia's presence on the Allied side also weakened Britain's attempts to restrain the Americans. The British wanted to hold back from invading France for as long as possible, letting the Russians wear down the Axis. But the Russians naturally wanted to see the pressure on them relieved by western intervention sooner rather than later. It was a testament to the political skill of Prime Minister Winston Churchill and his diplomats that the British had restrained their Atlantic allies as long as they had. But with two parts of their tripartite alliance calling for a new front, and with Britain's drained resources making the nation less influential within that alliance, it was time to give in to the inevitable.

There was another factor playing on the minds of the American and British planners, beyond balancing American boldness with British pragmatism. That was the future of post-war Europe. The alliance with Russia, while vital to victory, was an uneasy one. The governments of the western nations feared the spread of communism and the potential for Russian hegemony over large swathes of Europe. As the Russians gained momentum, and German defeat in the east became inevitable, the question wasn't whether the Russians would occupy parts of Europe when the war ended, it was how large those parts would be. The longer the Americans and British left it before opening up a new western front, the more of Europe would be dominated by communism in the aftermath. Outmaneuvering the Soviets wasn't as urgent a priority as defeating the Nazis, but it was important, especially to the belligerently anti-communist Churchill.

And so, the planning began for Operation Overlord, the Allied invasion of France. Over the winter of 1943-44, other options were gradually abandoned. Even an American scheme for a simultaneous landing in southern France was set aside, thanks to pressure from the British. The full weight of the available Allied resources in the west would be poured into this single operation. It would be carried out by a mixed force, predominantly American, British, and Canadian, but also featuring armies in exile from nations such as France and Poland.

While the details of the plan were a carefully guarded secret, the Germans knew that the Allies were going to invade. The question was where and when.

And so, on both sides of the Channel, forces were prepared for one of the most daring and decisive battles in history.

D-Day was coming.

Chapter 2 – Preparation

Among the first steps in preparing for D-Day was selecting the men who would lead the operations and creating a leadership structure for the combined military force. This was not a simple matter of selecting the most senior or most skilled officers. The operation would be led by a mixture of American and British men, many of whom were proud of their own national armies and reticent about working under foreigners. Operations in North Africa had shown that the historic experience of the British armed forces and the youthful power of the Americans led to two different flavors of arrogance that could clash at every level, from arguments in high command meetings to fist fights in infantry canteens. Pride, politics, and personalities all came into play.

The result was the selection of the American Dwight D. Eisenhower as overall commander for Operation Overlord. The diplomatic Eisenhower was popular with the American leadership, liked by Churchill, and through his leadership in Africa had proved he could manage the tensions between the forces of these two great powers.

The leadership of the initial stages of Overlord, beginning with the D-Day landings, went to the British General Bernard Montgomery, who was also commander of the ground forces. Because of their experience, British officers held many other senior posts, leading to tensions that Eisenhower had to balance. His job was made more challenging by senior air officers on both the American and British sides, who constantly resisted attempts to assert authority over them and to put military effort into an invasion. They believed their bombing campaigns could win the war and the plans for Overlord were a waste of effort.

Even before Eisenhower was in place, another important part of the preparation was underway – intelligence gathering. Early in the war, Britain had turned around its neglected military intelligence operation to become possibly the best intelligence gathering organization in the world. Now that apparatus was tasked with preparing for the invasion of France. Aerial reconnaissance flights began building up a picture of German forces and defenses in France, as well as the geography of the land they held. Holiday photographs of the French coast were collected from ordinary Britons, adding to the picture. German military signals were intercepted and decoded, including those from the high-level Enigma machines, secretly decrypted through the work of Polish and British experts. The French resistance fed what information they could into the mix, using contacts established by British special operatives earlier in the war.

Intelligence gathering continued right up to the invasion itself. Everything from supply orders to visits by senior German commanders gave the Allies information about the enemy forces.

Using this information, senior Allied commanders began planning for the campaign.

The biggest decision was where to land. They knew they were aiming for the coast of northern France, but where? Four major factors affected this choice: the distance across the English Channel to the site; how many men the beaches could hold; how heavily they were defended; and how far Allied air cover could reach to support the invasion.

The Pas de Calais was the closest landing ground and favored by some commanders for that reason. It held the major harbors of Calais, Boulogne, and Dunkirk, which could be used to unload troops and supplies. But that made it an obvious and heavily defended target, and a failed raid on Dieppe in 1942 had taught the British how costly such an attack could be. Brittany was too far away for a landing ground, so was quickly ruled out. A landing in the Cotentin Peninsula could too easily be contained by the Germans, preventing the Allies from breaking out of their initial bridgeheads.

Having eliminated most possibilities, the planners settled on the Calvados coast of Normandy. It was relatively poorly defended and had a series of broad beaches that would make excellent landing grounds. Having identified their target, the planners began outlining how they would take it.

American military planners had been working on this since 1942, but inevitably, there were arguments among the Allies. The phase line, which showed where American forces were expected to reach in the first 90 days, was removed from a map as the Americans did not want to commit to Montgomery's targets. It was a relatively minor issue, a line used to assess what supplies would be needed. But it took on symbolic significance as the big day approached and tensions rose.

The Allies could not wait until the plan was complete before assembling the forces that would carry it out. And so, in the spring of 1944, southern England became home to a vast assembly of armed forces, vehicles, and supplies. Hundreds of thousands of troops from across Europe and the English-speaking world gathered in previously quiet parts of the rural countryside. Alongside the Americans, British, and Canadians, there were Czechs, Frenchmen, Hungarians, Poles, and Jews from Austria and Germany. Almost every week, more Americans arrived. They all needed space to camp and to train, as well as supplies... With their chocolate and chewing gum, ordinary American infantrymen lived a life that seemed fantastically decadent compared with that of the war-weary and heavily rationed British.

In harbors along the south coast, 138 battleships, cruisers, and destroyers were mustered, along with 27 escorts, 2 submarines, 310 landing ships, and over 3,800 barges and landing craft. Together with minesweepers, motorboats, and supply ships, it was an incredible armada.

The troops didn't sit idly while they waited for the attack. Twenty-five miles of Devon countryside were cleared of its population for live-fire training exercises. Twelve-day courses prepared logistics officers for the complexities of supplying the invasion force. Maps of the real terrain were used for training, but with the names of places changed to maintain secrecy about where the landings were coming. Montgomery pushed the men hard to get them ready.

Hindsight would reveal gaps in this training. American troops rehearsed on the southern moors, the British on the flatlands of East Anglia. This terrain bore little similarity to the broken ground of the Norman Bocage, where winding roads, hills, and hedgerows provided plentiful cover and ambush points for defensive forces. The tactics practiced were generally those of the open order advance, rather than the infiltration tactics at which the Germans were skilled. But for all its limitations, a phenomenal amount was achieved in those months before the invasion.

Meanwhile, the less glamorous but no less vital work of logistics officers made the invasion possible. Ammunition, rations, vehicles, and medical supplies flowed across the Atlantic and into warehouses. Everything from biscuits to blood plasma was gathered and stored. Plans were made for how to distribute all these supplies to a huge army on the move through the fiercely contested territory.

The Mulberry harbors are the most famous part of this supply chain. Two prefabricated concrete harbors, they were built in large sections which could be towed across the Channel and then set in place at occupied beaches. This allowed men and supplies to be unloaded in places that had no port facility. It was thanks to this ingenious feat of engineering that the Allies could surprise the Germans by landing in an area without ports.

Alongside the supply ships, other communication and supply lines were prepared. The Petroleum Line Under The Ocean (PLUTO) was laid down once the Allies were established in Normandy, allowing fuel to be pumped from England to France. Telephone cables were also prepared, ready to be laid beneath the Channel, securely connecting commanders in France with those in London.

In the weeks and months leading up to the invasion, the Allies softened up the Germans for the attack. Much of this was targeted at infrastructure rather than directly tackling military targets. Attacks by Allied bombers and by the French Resistance weakened communication and supply networks in northern France, to prevent the Axis powers from bringing their strength to bear against the invasion. 1,500 of the 2,000 locomotives available in the region were taken out of action. Bridges across the Seine and the Loire were destroyed. Railway junctions and radar stations were also sabotaged. These attacks could not just be concentrated in the area around the invasion zone, as this would have given away the Allied plans, and so it took place across a broad area of northern France.

Ironically, the resistance of bomber commanders also helped pave the way for the attack. Reluctant to be diverted from their strategic bombing campaign against German cities, they contributed as little as they could get away with to direct preparations for D-Day. Meanwhile, the appearance of the American Mustang fighter to protect Allied bombers led to heavy losses among German aircraft, adding to Allied aerial superiority.

This bombing came at a cost. Twelve thousand Belgian and French civilians lost their lives – fewer than Churchill had expected, but still a tragic loss.

In the days leading up to the attack, preparations intensified. Minesweepers cleared the sea lanes for the invasion fleet. The Allies already had a tight hold on the Channel and had sunk half the U-boats trying to attack shipping in the region. The sea lanes were clear of German threats.

The original date for D-day – the launch date of the invasion – was 5 June 1944. Poor weather postponed it until the next day. And so, it was on the night of the fifth to the sixth of June the heaviest bombardment fell on the German defenders. As the fleet set out, 5,200 tons of bombs were dropped by heavy bombers on Axis defenses. As daylight came, medium bombers and fighters took over. Allied warships began pounding the German coastal emplacements.

Only now did the Germans begin to realize what they were up against. Achieving this surprise was an extraordinary part of the campaign. There were many more extraordinary acts to come.

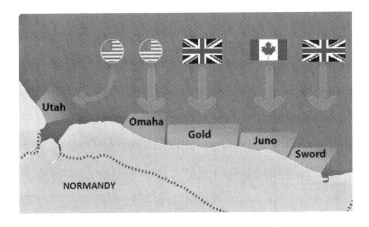

D Day attack plan. The five arrows are pointing to code names for five sectors of the allied invasion. These names are Utah, Omaha, Gold, Juno and Sword and will be discussed in greater detail later in the book.

Chapter 3 – Deception

In preparation for Operation Overlord, massive and ingenious deception operations were used to trick the Germans into believing the attack would not come in Normandy. Even after the attack began, these preparations would trick them into thinking it was a feint. Under the overall heading of Operation Bodyguard, several different plans, most famously Operation Fortitude, were used to trick the Axis commanders.

The Allied efforts were widespread. In the Mediterranean, an actor who looked like Montgomery was dressed up as the general and used to create a story the invasion might occur there. Diplomatic pressure on neutral Sweden, together with a supposed invasion force in Scotland, created the illusion an attack might come in occupied Norway. But while such actions did a little to spread German resources and sow confusion, they were nothing compared with the focus on the Pas de Calais.

This web of lies was easy to weave because it was so believable. The Pas de Calais was the attack route that made the most sense, thanks to the short journey across the Channel and the presence of several substantial ports. These facts made the lie easy to swallow, making it easier to deceive Hitler as to the Allies' true intentions.

Double agents were crucial to the success of this plan. Early in the war, the British tracked down every German agent in the country. Some were imprisoned, but others were turned, becoming British double agents. They were used to feed false information to Germany on several occasions. They provided a mixture of true and false information that made the lie of a Calais invasion convincing.

The most important double agent was a Spaniard named Juan Pujol Garcia, codenamed Garbo. The Germans were so convinced Garbo was a useful spy for them that Hitler awarded him the Iron Cross. Garbo fed the Germans information about the supposed Calais landing, which was scheduled after the real operation further to the west. After D-Day came, Garbo continued feeding false information to his contacts in Berlin, who continued to believe that the D-Day landings were not where the major invasion was going to take place. This subterfuge provided the Allied forces with extra time to consolidate their positions and press forward before the Germans committed any additional forces.

One of the most extraordinary parts of the plan was an imaginary invasion force, the First U.S. Army Group (FUSAG). FUSAG was created in 1943 as an administrative formation to help planning for the invasion and was initially led by General Omar Bradley. Bradley and his staff were moved to the headquarters of FUSAG, a force which existed only on paper.

FUSAG was notionally based in Kent, the natural staging ground for an army assembling to cross the Channel from Dover to Calais. Set-builders from filmstudios and theatres were brought from London to Kent, where they built a fictitious army. There were barracks and tents for the troops, and life-sized models of landing craft and tanks, all convincing enough to trick the limited aerial reconnaissance efforts of the Germans.

Radio signals were used to support the illusion. Military radio traffic filled the airwaves of Kent and was intercepted by German military intelligence as it drifted across the Channel. The Allies could tell this had been effective because they themselves were so much better at intercepting and decrypting German signals.

As the date of the invasion approached, a new leader was assigned to FUSAG. General George S. Patton was known for his aggressive and effective command style, which he had demonstrated against the Germans in North Africa. He had been removed from command in Italy due to disciplinary issues, and now he was put in charge of the imaginary FUSAG. The Germans rightly feared Patton. His arrival to command FUSAG therefore made it even more convincing and intimidating.

One of the most elaborate charades of the operation was used to bolster FUSAG. A badly injured Panzer officer, held in Britain as a POW, was being returned to Germany. He was told he would be travelling through Kent. There he saw armed forces being massed for an invasion and was introduced to Patton as commander of FUSAG. This provided the

Germans with eyewitness testimony for the existence of the force in Kent.

What they didn't know was the POW had been diverted through Hampshire, where the real armies were assembling, and where Patton had been brought specifically for the encounter. The troops were the D-Day armies preparing to attack Normandy, and Patton was a visitor like the German prisoner. The whole thing was a lie.

The activities of the Allied air forces were adapted to match the rest of Operation Bodyguard. Prior to Montgomery taking over, the planners for the invasion had concentrated aerial reconnaissance flights on the Norman coast, where the attacks were scheduled to land. Montgomery and his staff quickly changed this, extending aerial reconnaissance to cover the whole Channel coast, focusing on the area around Calais. This increased the effort needed to gather useful information but ensured these flights would not provide the

Germans with clues about where the attack was coming. Similarly, when they started bombing German communication lines in the build-up to the invasion, the air forces spread their effort over a wide area, maintaining the illusion the Allies were focused on the Pas de Calais.

All this effort would have been for nothing if German intelligence gathering had been more effective. But Allied efforts to counter it paid off. The turning and incarceration of spies at the start of the war ensured there were no German accurately reporting on events in Britain. Allied aerial superiority prevented effective German aerial reconnaissance, preventing the enemy seeing through the charade that was FUSAG.

The overall impact of this work was substantial. The Germans had to stretch their defenses to cover a great length of the French coast, preventing them from concentrating their resources where the invasion was going to fall. Hitler held the veteran Fifteenth Army around Calais for weeks after the invasion arrived, as he wanted them to fight off the strike by FUSAG.

Chapter 4 – The Commanders

Many extraordinary men led the Allied offensive on D-Day.

General Dwight D. Eisenhower

The man at the very top, Eisenhower was the supreme commander of the Allied Expeditionary Forces.

Born in Texas in 1890, Eisenhower was descended from German Mennonites, ironically a sect of extreme pacifists. He graduated from West Point in 1915 as an unexceptional new officer, coming in 61st academically and 125th for discipline out of a class of 164. He served in several posts before attending the Command and General Staff School, where he graduated first out of a class of 275, and then went on to the Army War College.

Eisenhower served in the Philippines as an aide to General MacArthur but left before the Japanese invasion in 1941. Back in the USA, he gained favor by planning the largest war games the country had ever run. When America joined the war, he was sent to join the planning team in Washington, where he was involved in early discussions about an invasion of Europe.

As overall commander of the Anglo-American invasions of North Africa, Sicily, and mainland Italy, Eisenhower had the experience for his role in Overlord. He lacked experience as a combat commander and was not an outstanding tactician. But he had the tact and political skill to manage the various strong personalities under his command, including Montgomery and Patton, as well as to delicately handle the French, who wanted to be treated as a major power despite their lack of military strength.

General Bernard Montgomery

Born in 1887, Montgomery went from school to the Royal Military College at Sandhurst. There he was demoted for setting fire to a fellow cadet and didn't graduate high enough to secure a coveted post in the British Indian Army.

Montgomery spent the First World War progressing through the ranks as an infantry officer and was severely wounded at the First Battle of Ypres. The horrifying losses he saw in Flanders made him determined never to use such senseless tactics. He concluded that serious life-long study was needed for military command, shaping his studious approach to leadership.

During the Fall of France in 1940, Montgomery led the 3rd Division in the vanguard of the British Expeditionary Force (BEF). Events there proved his skill as a leader, leading to senior positions despite his undiplomatic manner.

In August 1942, he was made commander of British forces in North Africa. He turned around the dispirited 8th Army and defeated Rommel at Alam Halfa and El Alamein, becoming a hero to the beleaguered British. When the Americans arrived, Montgomery's abrupt handling of them contributed to poor Anglo-American relations, giving Eisenhower his first experience managing Montgomery's awkward personality.

For Operation Overlord, Montgomery was commander of the ground forces and Commander-in-Chief during the initial invasion. His revision of the operational plans made Overlord the success it was and later earned him a promotion to Field Marshal. But his arrogance and his insistence all their successes were down to his own planning ensured that he would continue to antagonize colleagues throughout the war.

General Miles Dempsey

One of Montgomery's most trusted subordinates, Dempsey led a large part of the British and Canadian forces during the D-Day landings.

Born in 1896, Dempsey graduated from Sandhurst before becoming a British infantry officer in the First World War. Injured in a German gas attack, he had a lung removed. After the war, he served in posts around Europe and the British Empire, attended the Staff College, and continued his steady rise through the ranks.

As an infantry commander during the Fall of France, Dempsey led his men in several defensive battles. They played an important part in the rearguard during the retreat to Dunkirk.

Late in 1942, Dempsey was promoted to Lieutenant General and sent to join British forces in North Africa. There he caught the attention of Montgomery, becoming one of his most capable commanders. He helped plan the invasion of Sicily and commanded the airborne troops who spearheaded the attack.

Montgomery chose him to command the British Second Army, the main British and Canadian force, during the D-Day landings. Unlike his superior, Dempsey was modest and unassuming. Like Montgomery, he was an effective military commander.

Air Chief Marshal Sir Trafford Leigh-Mallory

Born in 1892, Leigh-Mallory was training to become a lawyer when the First World War broke out. He volunteered to join the British infantry as a private, quickly became a second lieutenant, and was put through officer training. After recovering from an injury, he joined the Royal Flying Corps, where he distinguished himself in the new field of aerial warfare.

Following the war, Leigh-Mallory stayed in the RAF. He received staff officer training and served in command, staff, and training posts.

In the late 1930s, Leigh-Mallory became commander of 12 Group, which he commanded during the Battle of Britain. An ambitious man, he was heavily involved in backroom politicking that was disruptive to the RAF. At times, he exaggerated the successes of his preferred tactics to further his career. His plotting paid off, and changes in the RAF saw him continue to rise through the ranks. He lobbied for a single overall commander to be created for Allied air operations during Overlord, and when this proposal was accepted, he was given the post.

Opinions of Leigh-Mallory varied. Montgomery liked him, as he provided the air support the general wanted. Eisenhower considered him capable but "somewhat ritualistic in outlook."

Admiral Sir Bertram Home Ramsay

Born in 1883, Ramsay joined the British Royal Navy in 1898. He quickly rose through the ranks and commanded several ships during the First World War.

Ramsay was brought back into service in 1939 by Churchill. Ramsay had retired in 1938. He oversaw Britain's naval defenses and in 1940 led Operation Dynamo, the evacuation from Dunkirk that brought home 338,000 Allied soldiers cut off by the advancing Germans.

Following Dunkirk, Ramsay grappled with the Germans for control of the Channel. He was involved in the invasions of Africa and Sicily, giving him the experience of seaborne landings.

Made Naval Commander-in-Chief for the D-Day landings, Ramsay coordinated a massive fleet of 7,000 vessels used to safely deliver 160,000 men onto the beaches on the first day.

Air Chief Marshal Sir Arthur Tedder

Born in Scotland in 1890, Tedder's early career was similar to Leigh-Mallory's. A civilian volunteer who joined the infantry at the start of World War One, he transferred to the Royal Flying Corps and stayed in the RAF after the war ended. He rose through the ranks, becoming Director General of Research at the Air Ministry in 1938.

Tedder was transferred to RAF Middle East Command in 1940. There, he provided air support for the evacuation of Crete and ground operations in North Africa. His tactical and administrative skills led to improvements in the British forces in Africa.

In 1943, Tedder took over Mediterranean Air Command. There he served under Eisenhower and took part in planning the invasions of Sicily and Italy. He came to Overlord with Eisenhower and served as Deputy Supreme Commander.

General Omar Bradley

Born in 1893, Bradley worked as a boiler maker before attending West Point in the same class as Eisenhower. Quiet and dependable, he rose through the ranks of the interwar American army, taking on command, training, and staff posts.

In 1942, Bradley oversaw the transformation of the U.S. 82nd Infantry Division into the first American airborne division. Graduating from West Point in the same class as Eisenhower, his classmates, and later his contemporaries, considered him quiet and dependable. He became the troubleshooter that helped to shape the Allied forces into a cohesive, fighting force. This was partly about building up the inexperienced American army, but it was also about keeping the peace between the Americans and British. He commanded II Corps in the last operations in Tunisia and in the invasion of Sicily.

As commander of the First United States Army (not to be confused with the fake First US Army Group), Bradley had overall command of the American ground forces during D-Day. Steady, capable, and discrete, he was excellent at reading a battlefield. Like Eisenhower, he helped to keep the peace in an operation sometimes troubled by strong personalities and the politicking prevalent in the air services.

Chapter 5 – The Men and Equipment

When looking at war, attention naturally drifts toward the commanders, the men at the top who make the big decisions and push the operation on. But it was the men on the ground who did the hard work of fighting on D-Day and beyond.

The British and American armies were quite different beasts, shaped by different cultures, traditions, and experiences of war. This shaped the sort of men serving in them.

Britain had a long tradition as a colonial power with a large standing army used to hold territory around the world. Britain's officer class had a certain prestige, even when commanding ordinary infantry units.

The professionalism of this military tradition had been hardened by the experience of war. The Battle of France and the retreat through Dunkirk; the failed intervention in Greece; years of fighting in North Africa; the Italian campaign –had all provided British troops with valuable battlefield experience. The pool of available manpower was more limited than in the American forces, and so men in all parts of the British military were likely to be repeatedly exposed to combat. Not every British soldier who landed on D-Day was a veteran, but the proportion of experienced men involved in Overlord was high.

The British forces included elements from the colonies and Commonwealth. For D-Day, this included a large force of Canadians. Like the British, the Canadians didn't have limitless resources, and so military prisons and hospitals had been scoured for men who could be put into action.

In the United States, which had long kept a small army and a policy of non-intervention, the military tradition was far less strong. There was pride in military service, but it wasn't as ingrained in the national culture. Specialist parts of the military were more prestigious than the infantry and had drawn of a disproportionate volume of the best men and resources, even during the early years of the war.

The bulk of the American forces were fresh-faced new soldiers, brought in as volunteers or through the military draft. A far smaller proportion of both men and officers had combat experience. Though the Americans recognized their limitations in this regard, there was little - they could do about it except to keep training the men pouring off the boats into southern England.

The main weapons of the infantry assaulting the beaches were rifles. The fundamental design of these weapons had changed little since the First World War, though they had become lighter and shorter. In modern warfare, a lot of the fighting was at short range, with men fighting in broken groups rather than massed ranks, and so weapons were optimized for this.

British soldiers carried the Lee-Enfield No.4 Mk I. The latest redesign in a series of related weapons. It was a bolt action rifle with a long sight for accuracy.

The Americans' main weapon was the M1 Garand Rifle. This was a more complex and expensive weapon than the Lee-Enfield, reflecting America's greater resources. A semi-automatic weapon, it automatically chambered a new bullet after each shot, avoiding the need to manually load as on a bolt action.

Some automatic weapons were also used, such as the M1 submachine gun and the Bren light machine gun. The lighter the weapon, the less firepower had, and so there was a balance between portability and firepower.

Armor was minimal, generally limited to a helmet to protect the head. The soldiers' fighting equipment was rounded out with bayonets for close combat and grenades for clearing out defended positions.

Aside from the infantry, the most important part of the ground forces was tanks. These became popular in the Second World War, with fast-moving armored formations sweeping across Poland and France. They were innovative, and allowed swift, decisive assaults.

The American M4 tank, known as the General Sherman, dominated. Crewed by five men and with a speed of 26 miles per hour, the Sherman went into production in 1941. It was produced in great numbers by the Americans, who supplied it to the British to serve alongside their vehicles.

Adaptations allowed tanks to make amphibious landings, coming off transport craft and straight up onto the beaches. A collapsible canvas screen was attached around the hull of a Sherman and filled with compressed air, allowing it to float. Two propellers drove it forward through the water. Once the tank landed, the canvas was deflated, creating a free firing view. This adapted vehicle was named the Duplex Drive tank.

Specialist military vehicles also played a part. For example, combat vehicles fitted with rotating flails could be used to clear mines. But it was the ordinary tank, and especially the Sherman, that would provide the heavy firepower to carry the Allies off the beaches.

In the air, the most renowned planes were still the Spitfires and Hurricanes with which the British had won the Battle of Britain. These swift, effective fighters had a fearsome reputation. But the aerial arms race was a fast-moving one, and it was a more modern plane that would prove decisive in Normandy.

The American P-51 Mustang had initially been a disappointing weapon. But when its Allison engine was replaced with a Rolls-Royce Merlin, its performance dramatically improved. It's great range, and combat ability let it effectively support the bombers attacking Germany and in doing so whittle down the German air defenses ready for D-Day. During the landings, it acted as both an interceptor, taking out enemy planes as they came for the Allied ground forces, and a ground attack craft, strafing German infantry with its six machine guns.

Amphibious landing vehicles were used to bring the infantry ashore. Experience in the Pacific had taught the Allies some valuable lessons in the use of these vehicles. It was best for men to unload from the front so they could advance up the beach quickly. But the moment the front armor dropped, those inside became vulnerable. Officers, therefore, had to take positions near the rear or risk becoming the first casualties and leaving their men without leadership.

Armed, trained, and ready, the Allied troops poured into their transport ships on the night of 5 June, ready to be carried across the Channel. But what came next didn't just depend on them. It depended upon the forces waiting on the other side of the Channel.

Chapter 6 – The German Defenses

The Germans had put huge effort into defending the territory they had conquered. Over the course of four years, from the fall of France to D-Day, they worked on a series of defenses meant to protect the entire coastline of northwest Europe, from the Pyrenees to the Arctic Circle. By June 1944, this Atlantic Wall included 12,247 fortifications, half a million beach obstacles, and 6.5 million land mines. The threats stirred up in the German imagination by Operation Bodyguard encouraged further efforts of this sort.

Anywhere the Allies landed, they would face beaches full of obstacles and explosives, guarded by armed men in concrete fortifications. This was particularly true along the Channel coast, as this was where Hitler believed an attack was most likely. He was determined to hold the Allies as they landed, prevent them from getting inland, and throw them back into the sea.

In August 1943, the defenses in Normandy were strengthened by deliberate flooding in the area around Caen. This was a tactic that had been used in the Low Countries during both World Wars, flooded ground impeding enemy movement. The developments around Caen gave the Allies pause for thought and were initially seen as a potentially serious hindrance to Overlord, then in its early planning stages.

Though few on either side were aware of it, the defenses in the target area were weaker than they might have been. As with many other German military construction projects, slave labor had been used in building the

Atlantic Wall along the Calvados coast. In some places, the laborers had acted as saboteurs, deliberately weakening the buildings they were constructing.

By late 1943, the troop formations manning these defenses were also being undermined. The war in the east was proving a huge drain on German manpower. As the year ended, 179 German divisions were serving on the Eastern Front, compared with 53 occupying the whole of France and the Low Countries. By the time the invasion came, this number had increased, but only slightly – from 53 divisions to 59.

With the Eastern Front an active warzone, it was unsurprising that men were syphoned off to fight there. Many of those who could be spared from fighting the USSR were seeing service in Italy, where the Allies continued to press against German defensive lines. Most of the toughest troops were already in action and so not available to man the Atlantic Wall.

Those units stationed in France were weakened, as the best troops were taken to fight elsewhere. Resources were not allocated to them as readily as to other units.

This began to change in November 1943 with Hitler Directive 51. Such directives had the full force of law and had to be obeyed by those who received them.

Directive 51 acknowledged an Allied invasion was coming in the west. Hitler believed if the planned Allied invasion could be stopped, the possibility of a western front being created would end. He could divert troops back to the east while superweapons such as V1 rockets bombarded England into submission.

Thanks to Directive 51, renewed efforts were made to train the troops, complete the defenses, and move soldiers west. Those sent from the Eastern Front brought with them combat experience, but the men were often weary and the units undermanned. There might have been more troops in June than there had been in January, but it wasn't a huge increase.

The quality of these troops was extremely variable. Many men who had not been selected to be sent east. Some were old, young, or suffering from injuries sustained in the East. Cynicism and poor spirits prevailed. Others were far more dedicated. The SS units, a politically driven elite within the German armed forces, were dedicated to their role and determined. Hitler depended on them. The Panzer tank forces were expected to provide the vital counter-strike against the invasion.

Alongside these German troops were many others who fought for the Third Reich not out of dedication to Germany but out of belief in Nazism or position to other governments. Russians, Poles, Indians, and a range of Eastern Europeans all manned places in the Atlantic Wall. They were less motivated to fight against the Americans and British than their comrades were. After all, theirs wasn't the nation with an empire at stake.

Overseeing the defenses was Erwin Rommel, known as the Desert Fox. A bold leader, Rommel made a name for himself during the First World War. On the Italian front, he led a detachment of men in an attack across the mountains around the Isonzo Valley, defeating and capturing forces that far outnumbered his own. Between the wars, he remained an infantry commander before becoming an instructor and the author of a best-selling book entitled *Infantry Tactics*.

Hitler was a fan of *Infantry Tactics* and made Rommel the head of his security unit. Rommel accompanied the dictator through the early days of the war and was rewarded with the command of his choice – leading a Panzer division.

At the head of his new tank division, Rommel led a decisive assault into France in May 1940, advancing at incredible speed. Leading from the front, he proved an inspiration to his men.

After France, Rommel transferred to North Africa, where he rebuilt Axis forces following a disastrous campaign by the Italians. His bold maneuvers, use of intelligence, and grasp of the potential of tanks saw the Allies driven back on several occasions. When Africa fell to the overwhelming weight of the newly arrived Americans, he took part in the defense of Italy before being moved on to plan the defense of France.

In November 1943, Rommel took over the Atlantic Wall. This led to a resurgence in work on the defenses. Four million mines were laid in four months. Anti-glider obstacles were set up along the coast. Training exercises were conducted. Rousing speeches were given. Rommel's presence was a grave issue for the Allies, partly because of his skill as a commander and because he reflected renewed German interest in bolstering northern France.

By June 1944, Rommel's presence and the activities triggered by Hitler Directive 51 had done much to bolster the German forces in Normandy. A week before D-Day, the 352nd Infantry Division, battle-hardened veterans of the Eastern Front, arrived to man the defenses around one of the landing beaches.

But there were limits on how much Rommel could achieve. Hitler's management of his subordinates through a strategy of divide and conquer was a hindrance to the smooth running of operations in France. None on the ground could claim overall control. Rommel was unable to give orders to reserves needed to stop the invasion. Hitler would not let Rommel place tank divisions close to the beaches, where the general believed they would be best placed, nor allow him to retreat and form a defensive line back from the coast. Hamstrung in his tactics, and with his belief in the potential for victory faltering, Rommel's moods became increasingly erratic.

As the invasion approached, timing took a hand. In early June, believing the Allies had missed their best opportunity, Rommel returned to Germany for his wife's birthday. While there, he was scheduled to meet with Hitler on 6 June to discuss the Atlantic Wall. At the same time, Sepp Dietrich, one of the best German tank commanders, was in Brussels, away from his 1st SS Panzer Corps. Most of the Seventh Army's senior officers were away from their posts, attending war games in Rennes.

At that moment, the Germans were vulnerable to attack.

Chapter 7 – The Paratrooper Landings

While most of the invasion forces were being loaded into their boats on 5 June, 24,000 paratroopers were waiting to take a far faster but no less dangerous journey across the Channel.

Two forms of transport carried the paratroopers to their landing points. Some were crammed into gliders, which were towed by planes to their targets before making rough landings in Normandy. This was dangerous and difficult work, and the casualty rate among glider pilots on D-Day was high, but it allowed heavier equipment and more troops to be brought in. The journeys of the other soldiers fulfilled the classic image of the paratrooper drop. Dozens of men crammed into noisy planes, barely able to hold a shouted conversation with their neighbors. Everything they needed was strapped to them, including support weapons and bulky radio sets. As they reached their targets, they would leap out in midair and parachute to the ground below.

As the first wave of planes swept in, many pilots became nervous about German anti-aircraft fire. The small number of planes lost shows that the German batteries were largely ineffective, but there was no way for the pilots to know this at the time. They swerved through the skies, throwing around their cargos of soldiers. Confusion arose as they tried to find their targets in the dark, and men were scattered across miles of French countryside, many far from their drop zones. Those who found the right place set up lights to signal the landing zones to later aircraft, making it easier to drop troops in the right place, but the operation got off to an inauspicious start.

One of the most daring parts of this plan was Operation Titanic. Despite its grand name, Titanic only involved ten soldiers, paratroopers from Britain's elite Special Air Service (SAS). What made the operation important was how and where they landed.

Just after midnight, the first of three Titanic drop teams landed on the Cotentin peninsula, miles from the rest of the army's drop sites and landing beaches. As well as the ten commandos, hundreds of specially made dummies called Ruperts were dropped. The Ruperts were crudely made, designed only to look like a paratrooper in the dark as they fell, and contained self-destruct mechanisms that would destroy the evidence of a fake after they landed. Five hundred of them parachuted down alongside the SAS men.

On the ground, the men let off fireworks and played gramophone records of gunfire, exaggerated to increase their volume. They set up lights to indicate a drop zone being prepared.

This distraction succeeded in drawing the Germans' attention. The German 915th Infantry Regiment, the main reserves near Omaha beach, headed away from the coast to deal with the threat of a non-existent paratrooper landing. Those ten SAS soldiers had an impact out of proportion to the size of their forces, but they also suffered disproportionate losses – only two of them made it home.

The main British paratrooper force was the British 6th Airborne Division. Consisting of 8,000 men. It was dropped east of Caen. It was to capture bridges across the River Orne, preventing German Panzer forces from coming in from the east and hitting the left flank of the seaborne forces.

The first wave of British paratroopers landed too far east. But their arrival came as a surprise to the Germans, giving them the initiative. They seized the village of Ranville and moved closer to the bridges, where they secured a landing zone. Two hours after the initial drops they were joined by troops in gliders, including anti-tank guns. Now close to the bridges, they captured all but one of them and fought off a counter-attack by the German 716th Division.

The remaining bridge at Troarn was a strategically important one, as it carried the main road between Caen, Le Havre, and Rouen. Seeing the need to deal with it, Major Rosveare assembled a team, explosives, and a jeep. They raced to the bridge and blew it up, cutting the last German route across that stretch of the river.

Out at the coast, 150 British paratroopers landed near the battery at Merville, which overlooked Sword beach. They attacked the battery, resulting in fierce hand to hand fighting in which half of the unit was lost. By the end, the battery was theirs, and they had destroyed the guns.

The 16,000 American paratroopers of the 82nd and 101st Airborne Divisions had a rougher time than their British counterparts. Their job was to land at the base of the Cotentin peninsula and stop any counter-attack toward the beaches by German troops stationed at Cherbourg. Like the British, they had to secure transport routes, in this case the causeways across the flooded ground behind the landing beaches.

Clouds and anti-aircraft fire scattered the 101st Airborne over a wide area. Some paratroopers landed in swampy ground, were dragged down by the weight of their equipment, and drowned before they could even get out of their harnesses. Only one in six of the men landed close enough to reach their rendezvous point. Less than half the gliders managed to hit the drop zone, and damage sustained in their landings led to the loss of valuable equipment.

The 82nd also struggled, though not as badly. After landing, they captured St Mére-Eglise on the Cherbourg road, the first town to be liberated by the Allies.

Scattered as they were, the paratroopers were unable to secure the bridges across the River Merderet that were among their targets. But they were determined to do the best they could in difficult circumstances. Men cut off from their units joined up with other formations. They attacked German troops wherever they found them, ambushing the enemy as they raced through the darkness, trying to work out what was happening. Lieutenant-General Falley, head of the German 91st Division, was among those killed by the wandering paratroopers.

Falley was killed while driving back to his headquarters from the wargames at Rennes. His movements were part of a frantic mass of activity as the Germans tried to work out what was happening.

The first paratroopers had landed just after midnight, but it wasn't until 1:30 a.m. that word of a possible invasion reached the German Seventh Army headquarters. At 3:00 a.m., word was sent to the military high command in Germany that an airborne invasion was underway, though the discovery of some of the Rupert dummies was creating confusion about whether this was real and what was happening. At 4:00 a.m., General Kraiss sent a cycle regiment in the wrong direction, tricked by the dummy paratroopers.

The absence of senior commanders added to the chaos. Tank formations that were crewed and ready by 2:00 a.m. were not deployed until 8:00 a.m. Self-propelled artillery was sent out for a counter-attack, only to be withdrawn as it headed up the road. The report that this was a major invasion was sent to Berlin at 6:00a.m., but critical reserves weren't released for another ten hours.

The invasion had begun. Though the paratrooper landings were chaotic for the Allies, this was nothing compared to the chaos on the other side of the lines. Despite its problems, D-Day was off to a good start.

Chapter 8 – Omaha

The most difficult and costly of the seaborne landings took place on one of the American beaches, codenamed Omaha.

Omaha had been chosen because of its strategically important location. That stretch of the coast needed to be taken to link the other American beach, Utah, in the west, with the beaches targeted by British and Canadian forces.

Due to its terrain, Omaha was an unpleasant choice. Three hundred yards of exposed sandy beach led up to a steep shingle bank that the troops would have to ascend. Beyond that, a sea wall and sand dunes were topped off with a 150-foot plateau on which the Germans had built defensive positions. At either end of the plateau, 100-foot cliffs blocked the way. The only exits from the beach were four ravines piercing the face of the plateau, and each of these was well defended by German troops.

To make matters worse, the bombing that preceded the landings was hindered by cloud cover. Forced to attack through the clouds, the American Liberator heavy bombers feared dropping their bombs too far short of the targets and so hitting the invasion fleet. To avoid this, they had erred on the side of caution. Hundreds of tons of high explosives had been dropped just beyond Omaha beach, but instead of striking the German forward defenses they had hit the fields behind them. The German defenses remained largely intact.

American soldiers who are wading onto the Fox Green section of Omaha Beach (Normandie, France) on the morning of June 6, 1944. Artist: Chief Photographer's Mate Robert F. Sargent.

The bombardment from air and sea stopped in time for the landings. But because of delays in the troops setting out, this created a gap between the bombardment and the assault, time for the Germans to recover and start firing on the approaching craft. As the American forces approached the shore, rocket ships opened fire to support them, but many of the shots fell short, hitting landing craft.

A north-westerly wind hit the coast as the landing craft approached. At least ten vessels were swamped by waves and sank, many of their occupants drowning. A similar fate met the crews of tanks as they left their transports too far off shore. On many of them, the amphibious gear failed, the vehicles sinking and taking their crews with them. Attempts to land artillery from amphibious craft also ended in disaster.

The failures in launching the tanks meant that the infantry hit the beaches without the armored support and so withstood the worst of the initial assault. There was no subtlety to the plan they had been given, no attempt to use maneuvers to seize the routes off the beach. It would be a headlong assault into enemy fire, much like those that had characterized the First World War.

The Americans decided to deploy their landing craft 12 miles off shore, unlike the less cautious British who chose seven miles. As a result, it took three hours for most of the attackers to reach shore. Drenched in sea spray and stepping in the vomit of their seasick comrades, it might almost have been a relief when the front gates opened and they could get out of the craft.

Any sense of relief swiftly turned to horror as they made their way onto the beach. German firepower from the cliffs above inflicted heavy casualties. Some men weighed down by 68 pounds of equipment, drowned before they reached the shore.

Reaching land, most men sought cover. Most of the obstacles on the beach remained intact, untouched either by the preliminary bombardment or by the engineers now struggling to make it safely to shore. And so, the obstacles designed to hinder the Americans became their shelters. Paralyzed by fear, men crouched behind what cover they could find, praying for deliverance from this nightmare.

The American forces were now pinned down on the beach. Machine-gun and artillery fire meant it took extraordinary courage to try to advance. They did not have the specialist anti-tank vehicles the British used, and most of the bulldozers meant to clear obstacles had been lost in the landings, along with 40% of the engineers trained to clear the way. Seeing their troops stuck in a bloody trap, Bradley and the other commanders began to worry about whether they would ever make it off the beach. Montgomery even suggested the remaining troops might be redirected to another beach.

Yet among all this mayhem, there were some small signs of progress. An infantry company from the second wave of landings was blown off course but reached the sea wall and picked its way through the minefield beyond.

Together with a group of Rangers, these men reached the plateau and stopped a counter-attack being launched against the men on the beach.

Further east, two battalions used the smoke from burning undergrowth and buildings as cover. By the time the German artillery found the range on their position, they were off the beach.

Throughout the morning, a traffic jam developed on Omaha beach, as newly arrived troops became trapped behind those already there. But those who had managed to press inland, away from the beach, started to chip away at the Germans in their pillbox positions. Not enough men had reached the high ground to achieve a breakthrough, but they at least divided the forces and attention of the defenders.

Seeing that extreme measures were needed to break through, General Huebner, commander of the 1st Infantry Division, called for a renewed naval bombardment. The ships sailed in so close rifle fire hit some of the ships. The navy began to shell the enemy positions. With the forces so close, there was a risk of hitting their own men. But if something didn't change, the troops on the beach were dead anyway.

While the Germans had the manpower and defenses to hold up the Americans, they lacked any reserves with which to launch a counter-attack. The 915th Regiment had been drawn off by the paratrooper landings. While the 352nd and 716th Divisions together represented more troops than the Allies had counted on being there, they were still outnumbered. As the heroism of individual American soldiers led to small breakthroughs and advances, there was no way to push them back. Bit by bit, the Americans began working their way up the ravines, until at last a breakout was achieved.

By 11:00 a.m., enough American troops had pressed forward inland to capture nearby Vierville. While some men kept up the fight against the defenses at the top of the plateau, others began to make their way cautiously off the beach. Bulldozers and explosives were turned to the task of clearing the obstacles and minefields blocking their way.

One by one, the German positions above Omaha beach were destroyed, either by the shelling of naval guns or by determined and courageous attacks by small bands of soldiers. At 1:30 p.m. Major-General Gerow signaled to Bradley the men previously trapped on the beach were making their way inland.

As the Germans responded to the growing crisis up and down the coast, they made a crucial error of judgment. The American forces at Omaha had achieved only a shallow beachhead and taken heavy losses along the way. If the Allies could be driven back into the sea, it was here. But instead of focusing on

Omaha, the German commanders hurried to bring their reserves to bear against the British and Canadians who had landed further east. One battalion of infantry was sent to tackle the American paratroopers in the Cotentin peninsula. Another lone battalion was sent to stem the tide of Americans pouring out of Omaha beach. It was not nearly enough.

By dusk, the beachhead stretched only 1,200 yards inland. The Americans had not reached their D-Day objectives, though they were now within a mile of them. They settled down to hold the ground they had taken.

The great cost and struggle that had gone into taking Omaha beach led to a change of plans in what was unloaded that night. Instead of quickly building up supplies on the beach to support the troops who had already landed, the bare minimum was landed to see them through the night. The focus was on bringing more troops ashore to keep up the fight. Exhausted sailors worked long into the night, bringing more of the fighting force off the transport ships and onto dry land.

At Omaha, the Allies had come closer to defeat than anywhere else in the D-Day landings. But perseverance and courage saw them through.

Chapter 9 – Utah

There was a huge contrast in the experience of the troops on the two American beaches, for both the attackers and the defenders. Utah was more orderly and far less costly for the Americans. But its end results, much like those on Omaha, were a disappointment for the ambitious Allied commanders.

German forces at Utah beach were far less substantial than at Omaha. As with so much about the defense of Normandy, this stemmed from a lack of understanding on the German side of what the Allies would want from the geography of their landing zones and how they would use the terrain to their advantage.

Behind Utah beach, flooded and marshy ground would constrict the movement of troops in from the coast. Only a limited number of causeways would allow tanks to move inland and men to make their way in without wading through deep waters. It was ground that could have been designed to slow down an invasion.

But Utah had critical advantages. It was a large enough beach to accommodate the landing of tens of thousands of men and their supplies, as well as tank and support vehicles. The flatness that contributed to the flooded lands beyond meant a relatively easy ascent up the beach. And strategically, its position near the neck of the Cotentin Peninsula would allow the Allies to gain control of the peninsula and the port of Cherbourg.

The relatively small force of Germans holding Utah beach was in for a terrible shock on the morning of 6 June. Three hundred and sixty Marauder medium bombers stormed out of the heavens, raining their payload down on the German emplacements. The Marauder was one of the best American bombers of the war, hard to take down and with heavy armaments for a plane of its size. The Marauders were followed by a remarkably accurate naval bombardment. Eighteen Allied warships lying off the coast opened fire, destroying many of the heavy guns and concrete bunkers the Germans were relying on. German troops pulled back into defensive positions, manned what heavy weapons remained, and waited for the inevitable assault.

The initial American assault came in four waves. The first was meant to be a formation of 32 amphibious tanks from the 70th Tank Battalion, followed by three waves of infantry. As at Omaha, the infantry was placed in their landing craft 12 miles off coast and suffered through a three-hour journey in vehicles best suited to short trips from ship to shore. As at Omaha, it was a salt-encrusted and often sea-sick force that reached the beach.

Better luck and weaker German resistance meant more troops did make it safely to the beach. Of 32 tanks, 28 made the journey from their transport craft intact, a far better result than in the disastrous tank landings at Omaha. But a strong headwind delayed their arrival by 20 minutes. Instead of arriving before the infantry, and so providing them with cover and support from the start, they landed after the first wave of troops had already hit the beach.

That first wave arrived at 6.30 a.m. Currents off shore brought the landing craft in further south than had been intended, leading to even weaker resistance. This was the most lightly defended part of the whole Normandy coast and the Germans had been suitably softened up. As the men waded 500 yards to the shore, only minimal fire hit them. Most made it safely onto the beach.

Then came the tanks. The shocked Germans saw machines rising out of the water, like so many sea monsters emerging from the ocean depths. Tank guns joined infantry fire, knocking out concrete defensive emplacements and the guns they held.

Desultory artillery and machine-gun fire hit the Americans as they advanced. The infantry made swift progress, taking on the few defenders and clearing the way for the further waves of troops as they arrived. Many of the Germans, seeing they were badly outnumbered, chose to surrender rather than fight on against overwhelming odds.

While the first waves of infantry advanced up the beach, engineers set to work clearing the way for the men and vehicles that would follow. They defused mines and blew up obstacles, creating a path the tanks could get through.

At Omaha, each thing that went wrong had led to more problems. The loss of engineers and bulldozers on the way to the beach meant they struggled to clear away the defenses. The defenses and loss of tanks hindered the advance off the beach to take out the Germans, meaning that the engineers and the rest of the men trapped with them took even heavier casualties.

At Utah, success bred further success. The ease of the landings and the advance up the beach made it easier for the engineers to do their job, making further advances simpler and safer. Within three hours of the first landings, paths had been cleared for tanks to drive up the beach, secure the causeways beyond, and support an advance inland.

Meanwhile, the American infantry had found five routes off the beach, one undefended ahead of them and four more at the western end, where the Germans put up little fight. They began heading inland.

While Utah had provided the easiest landing, it also provided the most difficult terrain for an advance away from the coast. The causeways funneled men and tanks down a couple of narrow routes. The Germans heavily defended the end of one of the causeways, destroying a bridge that was part of the route. Engineers had to carry out repairs and remove damaged vehicles before the tanks could complete their journey.

Many men were forced to sit and wait for hours, staying in what cover they could find in case of enemy fire. Rather than wait to join the narrow causeway advances, some infantry headed off through the flooded land. It was a slow and unpleasant journey as they waded along, weapons raised above their heads. The water ruined prized cartons of cigarettes. Engineers marked out paths for the infantry with white tape, but even so, some men stumbled into hidden ditches and almost drowned.

German resistance stiffened as the Americans headed further inland. But the paratroopers who had landed in the area, and with whom the Utah forces were meant to link up, created confusion and distraction among the Germans.

By the end of the day, forces from Utah had advanced six miles inland. They hadn't completed their task of linking up with the 82nd and 101st Airborne, nor had they reached all their objectives. But they had landed 23,000 troops on a defended coast, taking only 197 casualties in the process. More men were lost in vessels sunk by the Germans than in the fighting for the beach itself.

The Americans had one chaotic landing and one highly successful one. Further east, the British and Canadians were experiencing less extreme conditions as they made their landings.

Chapter 10 – Gold

Gold Beach was the westernmost of the British invasion beaches, the point at which the Anglo-Canadian forces would meet the Americans of the Omaha beachhead. A stretch of coastline between Port-en-Bessin in the west and La Rivière in the east, steep cliffs overlooked its western end. As a result, the actual landing zone ran from Le Hamel to La Rivière.

Gold Beach was reasonably well defended by the Germans. There were seven defensive strongholds, each designed to be held by 50 men, as well as two substantial but partially constructed artillery emplacements that provided shelter for heavy guns. As on the other beaches, a range of obstacles stood in the way of the men emerging from the sea. Land mines, anti-tank obstacles, wooden stakes, and metal tripods were combined with barbed wire to create a difficult and dangerous approach. Believing the Allies would arrive at high tide, reducing the amount of time troops spent advancing up the beach, Rommel ordered these obstructions be focused around the high tide line.

At 5.30 a.m., the naval bombardment began. Allied ships sitting off the coast battered away at the gun emplacements above Gold Beach, with light and medium bombers also contributing to the attack. Self-propelled guns aboard the landing craft added to the barrage, though these were not as effective as had been hoped.

Several of the German heavy guns were taken out, but some remained. The bombers failed to crack a gun emplacement at Le Hamel, leaving it free to fire on the western end of the Allied landings.

The remaining guns and gusts of wind made for a rough ride onto Gold Beach. Sea mines made things worse. Of five landing craft carrying the 47 Commandos to the beach, three were destroyed by mines, leaving the surviving commandos to swim for shore.

The landings began at 7.25 a.m., nearly an hour after the Americans began their landings up the coast. The tides had dictated when was best for each landing, preventing them from all coming at once.

Tanks were supposed to accompany the first landings, but this proved difficult. Rough seas meant the tanks had to deploy closer to land than had been planned and their arrival on the beach was delayed. The first wave of infantry thus had to manage without them, many taking cover behind pieces of the German beach defenses.

The tanks used on Gold Beach were more varied than those on the American beaches. While the Americans liked to use large numbers of identical vehicles, the British liked to experiment with specialist vehicles. As well as the armored bulldozers needed for clearing defenses, there were tanks with flamethrowers to burn out troops from well-defended positions and others with giant rotating flails which could be used to explode mines ahead of the tank, clearing a path for others to follow.

Self-propelled guns approached the beach, firing from their landing craft as they went. When they got near, gunners dressed only in underwear and gym shoes leapt into the sea to deploy mats referred to as "roly-polies", which the vehicles could drive up to get onto the shore. With German guns blazing and the wind threatening to drag their landing craft onto mines, the gunners struggled to maneuver the unwieldy roly-polies into place. Despite these efforts, many tanks became bogged down or were destroyed by German fire before they could advance up the beach, especially at the western end.

Engineers and mine-clearing tanks began clearing routes up the beach. Meanwhile, men ran from the exposed open sand into the greater cover provided by the dunes. As they progressed up the beach, they fought Germans defending trenches and pillboxes. Within a few hours, they were making advances inland.

Gold Beach saw one of the most extraordinary displays of courage on D-Day, and indeed throughout the war.

Sergeant Major Stanley Hollis was a member of the Green Howards, an infantry regiment from northern England. Veterans of the fighting in the Middle East, North Africa, and Italy, the Howards had impressed Montgomery with their courage and tenacity and so were chosen to be part of the first wave of troops to land.

As a member of D Company of the 6th Green Howards, Hollis led a detachment under heavy fire up Gold Beach. After fighting enemy troops hidden behind a hedge, they crossed a minefield and spotted a German pillbox on the far side. This was the source of the heavy fire that they and others in the area had been suffering.

Sten gun blazing, Hollis single-handedly charged the pillbox, drawing the enemy's fire away from his comrades in arms, and defeated the Germans inside. After taking a second pillbox, Hollis learned about a vital gun emplacement, which he led his men against.

As the Howards advanced inland, Hollis ran up against a group of well emplaced German soldiers. When an attack against them failed, he went back to retrieve two men who had been left behind in the retreat.

Even amid the other acts of courage on D-Day, Hollis's persistent presence in the heart of the action drew attention and he was awarded the Victoria Cross, the highest honor available to British service personnel.

On D-Day afternoon, Hollis and the Howards weren't the only ones heading inland from Gold Beach. British forces advancing from the beach took control of the road to Bayeux, seizing the village of Ryes. Though they didn't get as far as Bayeux itself, and like all the Allied forces they didn't reach all their D-Day goals, they made significant advances. Forces were diverted to taking out the Germans at Le Hamel, reducing advances in other areas.

Meanwhile, 47th Royal Marine Commando had a specific task for the day. This force of 420 men was to arrive on the beach at 9.25 a.m. and head out west. Their target was the small harbor of Port-en-Bessin, at the boundary with the American Omaha sector. Because the harbor was well defended from the seaward side, they would attack it from the south, securing it as a landing place for the Allies.

The Port-en-Bessin expedition got into trouble before it even hit the beach. Several of 47 Commando's landing craft were hit by mines, causing 76 casualties. Some men became separated from the rest. Those who remained gathered and headed for their target, but were slowed down by heavy skirmishes with Axis troops. By the time they reached the launch point for their attack, a ridge south of Port-en-Bessin, it was ten thirty at night and too late to continue. They dug in for the night. The next day, they would launch their attack, taking the town in two days of fighting.

The landings on Gold Beach had been largely successful. Though certain key targets for the day, such as Port-en-Bessin and Bayeux, remained in enemy hands, the beach had been taken, and significant progress had been made inland. 25,000 men had come ashore, of whom around a thousand had been killed or injured. They were ready to link up with the Americans in the west and so join up the Allied front.

But the most significant target, and the place of greatest German resistance lay beyond the other British beach. And between that and Gold lay the Canadians.

Chapter 11 – Juno

Responsibility for taking Juno beach fell upon the Canadian army. The size and prestige of the American and British military forces means that the Canadians have often been neglected in accounts of the Second World War. But just as in the First World War, they faced challenges as great as those of the other Allies, displaying every bit as much courage, skill, and tenacity as their comrades in arms. As at the other beaches, the naval forces supporting the operation were also a reminder of the remarkable international nature of the coalition facing Germany, with the Allied fleet including Canadian, British, Free French, and Free Norwegian vessels.

Juno was one of the more strongly defended beaches. The usual mass of obstacles blocked the way up the beach at the high-water mark. Behind them, there were strongpoints every thousand yards, involving machine-gun posts, artillery positions, and bunkers. These were defended by the 716th Static Infantry Division, a unit which was mostly made up of very young or old soldiers, but which was still considered better than average for a division of its type. Panzer forces and eastern European conscripts were stationed inland.

The Juno landing ran into difficulties before the men even hit the beach.

The usual bombardment by air and sea preceded the arrival of troops. This bombardment included the use of obsolete Centaur tanks carrying 95mm howitzers and providing covering fire from their landing craft. But the combination of landing vessels and the firing tanks turned out to be far less seaworthy than had been hoped. Scores of them sank, and only six made it to shore to support the infantry.

Meanwhile, a reef off the beach provided an obstacle to all the landing craft. The advance was delayed, and the pilots struggled to coordinate as they crossed the difficult waters.

When the infantry hit the beach, they landed amid the obstacles laid out by the Germans. They also arrived without the tank support they had been expecting, as the difficulties at sea meant many of the amphibious tanks and the specialist obstacle clearing tanks were held back.

Having deposited the troops, the craft were meant to pull out. But they became caught up in the German defenses, steel obstructions and mines preventing them from getting out. As more landing craft came in, mines damaged some, forcing the soldiers inside to get out and wade ashore. Of the first 24 landing craft, 20 were lost or damaged. For the whole morning, it was 90 out of 306.

Faced with rows of obstacles and barbed wire, under fire from the German troops in their defensive positions, the Canadians began advancing up the beach. Their experience varied hugely from one part of Juno to another. Some units came under heavy fire and quickly became worn down. Others had an easier time and could start tackling the obstacles in their way.

Meanwhile, the first tanks onto the beach opened fire on the German strongpoints, hoping to destroy tough concrete emplacements that had survived the preparatory bombardment.

In some parts of the beach, the Canadians became pinned down by German fire. At the east end, even the 100-yard run from the boats to the cover of the sea wall proved costly due to heavy enemy fire. The shortage of tanks meant that the infantry lacked the heavy support that they needed to advance. They couldn't clear out the Germans and so make the beach safe for obstacles and mines to be cleared and a path created for the vehicles. Troops became backed up on the sands.

Breakthroughs came in different ways in different places. Commandos risked heavy casualties to rush up the beach and into action. One of the supporting ships came in close to shore and hammered the defenders at the east end of the beach with its guns, providing a way off the beach. Demolition bombs, tanks, and other heavy weapons took out strongpoints, though often at a high cost.

By the early afternoon, the breakthroughs had been made and the Canadians were engaged with the second line of German defenses, inland from the beach itself. As they advanced, they ran into fresh difficulties.

Some units were held back by the loss of equipment on the way to the beach. Supplies had been lost with damaged or destroyed landing craft. Some bulky equipment had been abandoned as men struggled to make it onto the beach.

German snipers played a part. Placed in carefully chosen positions, they began picking off soldiers as they advanced. All the troops that landed on D-Day had to face a choice – whether to tackle isolated snipers, and so slow down their advance, or to keep moving, letting the snipers remain behind them and accepting the casualties this would likely cause. The Canadians kept moving on past, not letting these isolated assassins pin them down.

It was one thing to advance across a beach and through open fields. It was quite another to face the enemy in the coastal villages that dotted the landscape. These provided defensive positions for the German troops, with plenty of cover and hiding places. At Courselles, street fighting bogged down the advance through most of the afternoon. At St Aubin, it took three hours to drive out the last Germans. At Bernières, half an assault company was lost in the hundred-yard advance from landing points to the village, and the enemy clung tenaciously to their position until they were eventually outflanked.

At Tailleville, tanks advanced through the village, smashing German positions. But they hadn't counted on the complicated network of emplacements the defenders had built underneath the village. The Germans used these bunkers to repeatedly outflank the Canadian infantry. It was only after seven hours of fighting the village was cleared.

Having fought their way off the beaches, the Canadians went on to make the deepest advances of D-Day. Follow-up units moved past the tired troops of the first landing waves and used the routes they had established off the coast. Pushing on to their objectives, they got seven miles inland, further than any other Allied troops. They reached the road between Bayeaux and Caen, a critical artery for traffic in the region, and got within three miles of

Caen, where they linked up with the British 50th Division.

Meanwhile, the assault troops around the beaches mopped up the remaining German resistance. Snipers continued to harass the Canadians until nightfall, by which time they were left isolated far behind Allied lines.

As night fell, Canadian forces dug in along a line inland from Juno beach. Their landings had been among the most successful of D-Day, despite the ineffectiveness of the preparatory bombardment and the heavy losses taken in some parts of the beach. They had sustained around 2,000 casualties. In return, they had smashed the German formations facing them, broken through the Atlantic Wall and its defensive formations, and linked up with the British at one end of their line.

Things were only going to get tougher for the Canadians. Their achievements, and those of the British to their east were drawing the attention of the Germans. There would be no easy advance on Caen.

Chapter 12 – Sword

Sword Beach, the easternmost of the landing zones, was one of the British targets. Lying closest to the city of Caen, it was a vital anchoring point for Montgomery's strategy for the following weeks. It was also the sector of the line that would most obviously demonstrate the over-ambitious nature of Allied goals for D-Day.

Sword had the same sort of defenses as the other beaches the Allies landed on. Landmines, stakes, and concrete blocks designed to stop tank advances all littered the flat, open beach, interspersed with occasional pillbox defensive emplacements. Behind that were 20 strongpoints, some containing artillery. Machine-guns and snipers were installed in former tourist homes lining the shore.

What made this part of the line different was the German reserve force based near Caen, nine miles from Sword. The 21st Panzer Division, a 16,000-strong force of tanks, mobile troops, and anti-tank troops, held positions either side of the River Orne. If they could be mobilized and brought to the fight, they could make a huge impact on the British advance.

The aerial and naval bombardment of the defenses at Sword Beach began at 3:00 a.m. The effort was concentrated around Hermanville-sur-Mer, where the landing craft could most easily reach the beach.

As the Allied bombardment pounded the German positions, troops started heading to the beach. In the forefront were the tanks, including the specialist vehicles the British referred to as "funnies," such as the mine destroyers and flame throwers.

A mile from the beach, German shells started hitting the landing craft. The craft pressed on, some in dramatic style. A bugler sounded the General Salute as he passed the command ship.

The British had an incredibly detailed plan for the waves of troops to hit the beach. First would come the amphibious tanks at 7.25 a.m. Five minutes later, landing craft would deposit specialist engineering tanks into the shallows, where they would emerge onto the beach. The first wave of infantry would arrive seven minutes later, the next thirteen minutes after that, and so on through the early hours of the landing.

The operation got off to a good start. The first waves arrived on time. As mortar and machine-gun fire rained down around them, sappers set to work demolishing obstructions. Flail tanks whipped the sand, safely setting off mines before anyone was close enough to be caught in the blast. The specialist tanks also showed they could be useful in a more general role, using their guns to take out German gun emplacements.

Some of the first men off the boats were hit immediately. But these formations who took point didn't suffer as heavy casualties as others who followed behind, pushing past them to launch advances in the face of heavy enemy fire.

The mine-clearing tanks began using their flails when they hit the high-water mark and kept going until they were off the beach. This cleared paths for others to follow. Amphibious tanks cleared the beach of any tough positions and then drove up into the dunes, where they became involved in heavy fighting.

Despite the successful start, a schedule as complex as the British landing one inevitably began to fall behind. There was no way every wave could land on time in the face of opposition. The beach became clogged with men, vehicles, and wreckage. Throughout the day, German mortars and artillery from further inland bombarded the men waiting to get off the sands and into action.

Meanwhile, a single courageous French girl waded into the blood-stained waters and helped wounded soldiers out of the shallows.

Despite German resistance, the British secured Sword Beach in less than an hour and headed inland with remarkable speed. By nine in the morning, the men of the 1st Battalion South Lancashire Regiment were over a mile inland at Hermanville.

Montgomery's aim for this force was focused on Caen. They were to advance to the city, engage with the Panzer forces there, and hold them over the following days while the Americans secured the Cotentin Peninsula. This meant a speedy advance to ensure the Panzers were fully occupied.

Commando units and men of the East Yorkshire Regiment set out from the beach to take Ouistreham and Lion-sur-Mer. Tanks rushed from the coast to pre-planned rendezvous points, past shocked Germans cowering in shell holes. Though they had fought their way through the first line, they still faced opposition. Snipers fired at exposed men. German guns of the 1716th Artillery Regiment rushed up to launch a counter-attack at Lion-sur-Mer.

The counter-attack at Lion was briefly successful. The British had not yet brought up heavy weapons and so were vulnerable to the German artillery. The Germans captured a group of British prisoners and were amazed at the quality of their supplies compared with those in blockaded Germany. But the success was short lived. The Allies brought up more troops, and the Germans were pushed back.

Their level of success surprised the British troops. They had been trained to fight on the beaches. Now they were inland, facing different conditions from those they had most prepared for. The success was gratifying but at times bewildering.

At 11:00 a.m., troops began gathering for the advance to take Caen. The initial force was meant to consist of the 2nd King's Own Shropshire Light Infantry (KSLI) and a group of tanks from the Staffordshire Yeomanry. The KSLI gathered in an orchard outside Lion, threw away their no longer needed maps of the area around the beach, and marched to Hermanville to meet the tanks.

But the tanks were stuck. An unexpectedly high tide, combined with many support vehicles on the beach, had obstructed their advance. An hour after the group was meant to set out, the KSLI started marching for Caen alone, with the tanks set to catch up later.

Meanwhile, other troops were fighting to take out two German strongpoints labelled "Morris" and "Hillman." Hillman proved particularly tough, and the 1st Battalion of the Suffolk Regiment took heavy casualties there. Looking for a way to take the position, an engineer discovered tanks could safely cross the minefields. The vehicles used explosive charges to breach the defenses, leading to the strongpoint's capture.

The KSLI fought a series of small but fierce engagements as they advanced toward Caen. Late in the afternoon, now accompanied by some of the promised tanks, they reached Biéville and again overwhelmed the Germans, this time through a flanking maneuver.

It was here, at Lebisey wood, that the British advance on Caen stalled. The first formations of the German 21st Panzer Division joined the fight. The leading company of the KSLI took heavy casualties, including the loss of their commander. Under heavy fire, they halted around 6:00 p.m. and dug in for the night. The leading company pulled back, disengaging from the Germans to take shelter with the rest of their regiment.

On a hill above Lebisey, the German General Marcks saw that, while he had halted the advance on Caen, the situation was dire. The Allies had landed in force and were pouring more troops into their bridgehead. Presciently, he said if the British could not be thrown back into the sea, Germany would lose the war.

He launched a counter-attack.

Led by Marcks himself, a German Panzer formation rushed north across open land, heading for the gap between the British and Canadian landing zones. If he could exploit that weak point, maybe he could drive the invaders back.

It was a desperate and ineffective gamble. As the Germans reached the Sherman tanks of the Staffordshires on a hill near the Caen road, they immediately lost 13 of their own tanks. By the time they reached Lion-sur-Mer, only a fragment of Marcks' original force remained. Seeing Allied gliders coming into the east, they feared they would be encircled. They withdrew toward Caen.

The result was one of mixed fortunes. The British hoped to take Caen on the first day. It was a strategically important objective, and now it was defended by the remains of Marcks' force. On the other hand, the German force lost 70 out of 124 tanks in their futile counterattack, severely weakening the defensive formation.

With minimal tank and artillery support, taking Caen on the first day was never a realistic objective for the KSLI. Given the Panzer forces in the vicinity, it might never have been plausible for the British at all. At Sword, as at the other landing zones, D-Day ended with key aims unfulfilled.

The Allies had achieved an extraordinary thing, securing a beachhead in Normandy in the face of Rommel's carefully prepared defenses. But the Germans had fought well.

As night fell and the two sides dug in, the question became, where do we go from here?

Chapter 13 – The Resistance

While the foreign soldiers landed on their north coast to liberate them, the people of France were not sitting idle. While most had no idea what was happening on the Norman coast, a significant minority knew the invasion was coming. They leapt into action to support it.

For the 100,000 men and women of the French Resistance, the call to action had come.

The Resistance first emerged in the immediate aftermath of the fall of France in 1940. Though most French people turned to the government in ostensibly free Vichy to keep their nation alive, others chose different paths. For some, this meant exile and joining General Charles de Gaulle's Free French forces in England. For others, it meant resisting the Germans from within, forming cells of freedom fighters who sought to cast out the Nazi-led invaders.

Initially, much Resistance activity consisted of attacks on German soldiers, the most direct and obvious way of hurting the occupiers. But this brought acts of sometimes terrible retribution down upon the heads of the French. And so, in time, the Resistance turned to less direct tactics. Attacks focused on the infrastructure supporting the German troops. Supply and communication lines were attacked. Equipment was sabotaged. The men and women carrying out these attacks were still risking their lives, but the penalties for their communities, if they were caught, would be less severe.

The growth and increasing coordination of the French Resistance was supported by the work of the Allies. Britain's Special Operations Executive (SOE), America's Office of Strategic Services (OSS), and De Gaulle's Free French forces sought to work with resistance cells. They linked up with existing groups, recruited new ones, and provided supplies. They gave them radios to stay in contact with each other and the outside world.

The Resistance was never just a means of attacking the Germans. They were also a valuable source of intelligence, helping the Allies to keep on top of events in occupied France, and a part of the escape networks that helped downed pilots and men who escaped from POW camps to get out of Axis territory.

One of the most important channels of communication was Radio London. This station broadcast from Britain for an audience on the occupied continent. It sought to provide a propaganda tool against the Axis and to keep the hopes of freedom-loving Europeans alive. It also provided a way to send messages to resistance members without them needing powerful and cumbersome two-way radio sets. Resistance groups provided phrases for the authorities in Britain. When these phrases were included in the "personal messages" section of a Radio London broadcast, that told resistance cells the time had come for specific events, such as supply drops.

By the time of D-Day, the Resistance had grown massively from its original roots. Hitler's war against the USSR had put pressure on German industry, and a labor draft had been introduced in France to provide manpower. This led to greater resistance than before, as the French sought freedom from such measures. As Overlord prepared to launch, over 100,000 people were part of the resistance network.

The Americans and British did not entirely trust the Resistance or even the discretion of their Free French allies. De Gaulle was only told about D-Day two days in advance. At the start of June, the Resistance were informed, by a signal from Radio London, that the invasion was imminent.

In the months leading up the operation, the Resistance had gone into overdrive, attacking German infrastructure, in particular railway engines. On the night before D-Day, a fresh signal from Radio London told them now was the time to go all out.

The signal informed the Resistance an invasion was coming, but not the location. They sprang into action, attacking transport and communications networks that could aid the occupiers. Five hundred and seventy-seven railroads, 30 roads, and 32 telecommunications sites were destroyed. The ability of the Germans to counter the landings was severely hampered by the infrastructure damage and acts of armed insurrection across France.

Just before D-Day, the Allies began a new form of coordination with the Resistance.

Jedburgh teams were three-man groups of uniformed Allied soldiers, one of them always French. They were parachuted into France with radio equipment, with the mission of joining up with Resistance groups. They helped to encourage and coordinate the Resistance, who was now officially brought under the wing of the Allied military.

The Resistance helped to make D-Day a success. But many members lost their lives as they responded to the signal only to find the Allies were weeks or even months away from reaching them with support. In the days that followed, they were active close to the battle lines, joining with regular Allied forces in a fight to free their country.

The beaches had fallen. The Allies were moving inland. The Resistance was rising ahead of them. But the battle for Normandy had only just begun.

Chapter 14 – Advance

As dawn rose on 7 June 1944, Allied forces sat in four distinct pockets on the Norman coast. The Canadians linked up with one of the British beaches, but other than that, each landing force was on its own. The longer they stayed separated from each other, the more time each group spent without the full support of the others. They were the more vulnerable for it.

One of the biggest challenges the Allied troops faced over the following weeks was the Bocage, the distinctive scenery of that part of France. Frequent hedgerows, sunken and winding roads, and tall earth banks all contributed to making a landscape that favored the defender. German guns, tanks, and infantry dug in using camouflage to hide and catch the Allies by surprise. In a single engagement, German tank ace Michael Wittman and his unit took out 27 British tanks in fighting at Villers Bocage, most of them destroyed in the initial ambush in which Wittman drove out of cover and down the length of a British formation, destroying the tanks as he passed.

While circumstances on the ground favored the Germans, those in the air were on the Allies' side. They had superiority in the air, allowing them to bomb German formations as they tried to reach the front. Close to the coast, this bombing was reinforced by bombardment from Allied ships, which could fire up to 16 miles inland. As the Allies moved away from the coast, they lost this cover but gained better close aerial support, as they established airbases close to the front lines.

The result was a steady Allied advance. The Germans could not muster a substantial counterattack, as Allied aircraft attacked any large formations they saw on the roads. But the Allies could not make swift breakthroughs, as they were bogged down fighting hedge-to-hedge and house-to-house to advance.

On the day after D-Day, a German SS Panzer force tried to launch a counter-attack. They were destroyed before they even reached the front.

While this attack was being thwarted, the British and Canadians finished linking up into a single front. The following day, Royal Marines captured Port-en-Bessin, and the day after that, the British linked up with the battered American forces at Omaha Beach. American paratroopers continued to gather together, becoming an increasingly coherent and effective force. But the Americans were struggling to bridge the gap between Omaha and Utah. It wasn't until 12 June, with an American victory in fierce fighting at Carentan, that the beachheads were all connected. The

Allies now held a single swathe of territory 15 miles deep and 60 miles long.

Allied air attacks prevented the Germans from mustering a substantial force in the region. Bombers attacked trains travelling west, stopping troops long before they reached the front. SS Panzer Divisions hastily summoned from the Eastern Front were smashed before they even reached the combat lines.

The Allies had no such problems. Tens of thousands of men were ashore, and still more were coming. The number who came through the Mulberry harbors would be counted in the millions.

Supply lines to Britain were almost ruined on the 19th when the fiercest storm in 50 years tore its way up the Channel. The Mulberry harbors were smashed, one of them beyond repair, though the one at Arromanches was made functional using parts from the ruined harbor. A dozen ships were sunk, and hundreds were blown onto the shore. The

Allies were left short of food and ammunition, their air cover grounded by the bad weather.

But by then Germans were well established in defensive positions. During their brief window of opportunity, no counter-attack emerged.

Having finished linking up, the Americans focused on taking the Cotentin Peninsula. The main strategic target there was the town of Cherbourg, which would give the Allies a deep-water harbor.

On 17 June, the Americans completed their advance across the neck of the peninsula. Three days later, they were within striking distance of Cherbourg. The German units there were tired and demoralized, but the commander of the garrison, Lieutenant General Karl-Wilhelm von Schlieben, refused to surrender. Instead, he sent his troops to destroy the harbor facilities so they would not fall into Allied hands.

On the 22nd, the Americans launched their attack on the city. Progress was slow at first, as the Germans were well dug in, defending concrete pillboxes and bunkers. The tipping point came on the 26th. That day, British commandos stormed the German naval intelligence headquarters, while American forces took Fort du Roule, which dominated the city. Von Schlieben was captured, and any organized defensive effort ended. The last Germans in the town were defeated on the 1st of July.

As planned, the Americans had taken the Cotentin Peninsula and were moving beyond there to advance west and south. But the British and Canadians remained stalled outside Caen. There, the Germans clung tenaciously to defensive positions around the city.

On 26 June, Montgomery launched a massive attack on Caen. Using devastating artillery power, the Allies took the critical high ground at Hill 112, south of the city. The following day, the Germans massed as many tanks as they could spare, some from the battered forces brought from the Eastern Front, others brought up from the south of France. They counterattacked at Hill 112, triggering a merciless five-day battle that saw a nearby river clogged with dead bodies.

Behind the German lines, political divisions made it hard to coordinate the military effort. Hitler's strategy for managing his subordinates meant there was no one in clear command of the forces in the region. His personal interventions were often misguided and made it difficult for commanders to effectively fight the war. Some of them, realizing the war effort was doomed, wanted to seek a negotiated peace with the Allies. Hitler refused to even consider the option, and so they began plotting an unsuccessful attempt to assassinate and replace him.

July brought heavy rain and with it bad memories. American, British, and French forces were once again bogged down in a slow, grinding war against the Germans amid the mud of northern France. Inevitably, it reminded people of the First World War, and some worried this would turn into another stalemate. In Britain, the sense of excitement that had greeted D-Day began to fade.

The Allies needed to break out of the patch of northern France in which the Germans had them contained. They began hatching a plan.

For the breakout to work, the Allies needed to ensure the British and Canadians under Montgomery were fulfilling their original purpose of occupying the German armored forces. This objective combined with the still incomplete objective of capturing Caen, resulting in a renewed attack on the city.

Two thousand, five hundred tons of bombs were dropped on Caen by the RAF, softening up the defenders ready for a big attack. The Canadians took heavy casualties assaulting the airfield at Carpiquet. The British invaded the northwest districts of the city and took them in two days of street-to-street fighting.

They attacked Hill 112 again, suffering heavy casualties to take the high ground.

On 17 July, a British Spitfire strafed the car of General Rommel as he returned to his headquarters. Rommel was severely injured. He was taken to the hospital and later committed suicide after being implicated in the plot to kill Hitler. The commander of the Atlantic Wall and one of the most dynamic leaders in the German military was gone.

The next day, Montgomery launched Operation Goodwood and Operation Atlantic. These two offensives saw the British and Canadians push hard against the Germans in and around Caen. Bitter fighting followed, and by the end, the devastated city was in Allied hands.

Montgomery's approach at Caen has been criticized by many historians, who argue his tactics led to unnecessarily high losses. The battle was certainly costly for the British and Canadians. But in a broader strategic sense, it achieved its objective. All the available German armor was being poured into holding the city. To the west, where General Bradley was commanding the American ground forces, there was not the same tough armored opposition.

By late July, the Allies held a substantial bridgehead in northern France. Now it was time to go beyond that sector.

It was time for a breakout.

Chapter 15 – Breakout

Throughout the campaign so far, one figure had been notable for his absence.

General George S. Patton was one of the most controversial commanders in the U.S. Army. Bold, determined, and skilled, he had risen to prominence as a tank commander. He had led American forces to successes in North Africa, where he became a hero to many and a terror to the Germans.

Patton's strong personality could make him a liability as well as an asset. He repeatedly clashed with other commanders, especially Montgomery. During the invasion of Italy, his physical and verbal abuse of a shell-shocked soldier created a storm of outrage that saw him deprived of his command.

But Patton was too popular and skillful a commander to be kept on the bench forever. During the build up to D-Day, the Allies used his presence to add weight to the illusory First U.S. Army Group without giving him the responsibility of command. Now the fighting was on, and they needed decisive action, he was exactly the sort of man they wanted at the front.

On 6 July, Patton arrived in Normandy. Bradley, previously his subordinate, was now his superior and had summoned him to lead a swift, hard strike that would break through the German lines, drive south, and then head east, catching the enemy by surprise. Hidden away in a camouflaged bivouac in the Cotentin Peninsula, Patton began work on assembling the U.S. Third Army, which he would command for this expedition.

On 25 July, the Americans began Operation Cobra. Three thousand bombers dropped 4,000 tons of napalm, high-explosives, and fragmentation bombs on a five-mile stretch of the German lines near St-Lô. Around 70% of the German troops ended up out of action because of the bombing – dead, wounded, or too traumatized to fight.

Into the ruins of the German lines, the VII and VIII Corps of the U.S. First Army began their advance. Isolated groups of German soldiers held out stiffly against them in a landscape of charred ruins and craters. As they were forced to withdraw, the Germans left minefields and booby traps behind, inflicting further casualties.

After the first day, the pace of the advance started to improve. There were fewer Germans left to resist. Hitler had ordered them not to retreat, preventing them from making a tactical withdrawal that might have held up the American advance.

The Americans took Coutances on 27 July and Avranches on the 30th.They were making progress, but this was still not the main event.

On 30 July, Bradley unleashed Patton. The Third Army poured through the gap created for them by the VII and VIII Corps.

After passing Avranches, the army divided. Part of the force headed west, while the rest swung southeast.

The western force went into Brittany. There, they faced only minimal opposition from the Germans. They occupied most of the region and reached the west coast ports of Brest and Lorient. Their presence distracted the Germans, who started sending troops west to tackle them, only to realize that this was not the main thrust of Patton's advance.

That main thrust was led by the 4th Armored Division and Patton himself. They pushed south and east, crushing German opposition along the way. The enemy was left uncertain about what was happening or how to react.

Until they knew where Patton was going, they did not know how to respond. The speed of his advance and the disruption to their communication network made it nearly impossible to work that out.

Assuming that Patton was headed for Paris, the Germans moved troops to counter such an advance. But his intention was different. He was heading southeast, sweeping around the German forces ready to cut them off.

The German Seventh Army, led by General Von Kluge, now lay in the jaws of a trap. Patton's relentless advance had been a massive flanking maneuver that threatened to cut them off from the south.

Hitler, who was 800 miles away in his Wolf's Lair headquarters, finally recognized the difficulty his forces were in. He began giving orders meant to save them from destruction. But so far from the action, he had a poor grasp of what was happening on the ground.

First, he ordered Von Kluge to move four armored divisions from the fight against the British to the American front. But the British had been successful in their aim of thoroughly pinning down the German troops. It took days to disengage from the enemy and extract the Panzers.

Meanwhile, four divisions of the Fifteenth Army were brought around from the Pas de Calais. Hitler had been reluctant to let go of the idea that the Allies were still planning a second invasion there and armored forces had been held in reserve ready to fight that non-existent invasion. But Patton's advance made it clear that the D-Day landings and what followed had been the main event. This was no distraction, no feint, no half of a two-part plan. This was the Western Front, and by holding back resources, Hitler had given the Allies an opportunity to shape it.

Hitler's plan was to launch a counter-attack at Avranches, the site of the gap through which the Americans had emerged. If he could close the gap, then he could isolate Patton, cut off his supply lines, and end his advance.

It was a fine idea in theory but not in reality. The German commanders on the ground advised against such a scheme. They did not have the resources for an effective counterattack against the Allied armies. Allied air power alone would provide a significant hindrance to the scheme.

But Hitler was not to be deterred. Swift, decisive strikes had brought success in the past, beating the numerical odds. They could do it again.

The plan began to fall apart on the way to Avranches. Two infantry and five Panzer divisions ran into an American division at Mortain. Though outnumbered, the Americans fought hard and held their position, delaying the Germans long enough until Allied reinforcements arrived. The Germans were halted.

Hitler was still insistent that Von Kluge should counterattack, but Von Kluge was making other plans. He saw that he could not win where he was and the best long-term hope for Germany lay in preserving the forces he had. He began planning for a withdrawal.

On 8 August, Patton reached Le Mans, far south of the main beachhead. From there, he headed almost directly north, into the rear of Von Kluge's army.

On the same day, the Canadians launched Operation Totalize. In a costly but successful offensive, they punched through the German forces south of Caen and pushed toward the city of Falaise. Like so many offensives, it was not as successful as the commanders hoped, but it threatened to cut the German Seventh Army off from the east.

On the 13th, Patton reached Argentan, not far south of Falaise. On the 14th, the Canadians launched a fresh offensive near the city. Von Kluge's forces were surrounded on every side, with only an 18-mile gap between Patton and the Canadians offering the prospect of retreat to the east.

Von Kluge ordered the retreat, in direct contravention of Hitler's orders. Axis troops began streaming through the Falaise gap.

Inside the isolated pocket of Germans, things looked bad. The French Resistance destroyed some units. Others surrendered to the advancing Allies.

By the 17th of August, the gap was only eleven miles wide. The next day, it was six miles wide, and the Allies were launching relentless air attacks, destroying anyone who tried to escape. On the 21st, American forces in the south met up with Canadian and Polish troops from the north, and the gap was closed.

Von Kluge was relieved of command and recalled to Germany. By now, he had not only disobeyed Hitler's orders, but he had also been implicated in a plot to assassinate the dictator. Rather than face his leader's fury, he committed suicide.

Ten thousand Germans were killed in six days of fighting in the Falaise Pocket. Fifty thousand were taken prisoner. In total, the Germans lost 400,000 men in Normandy, half of whom were taken prisoner. The Allies lost nearly 209,672 men, 36,976 of them were killed.

The remains of the German army were fleeing for the border. Operation Overlord had been a success.

Conclusion

On 19 August, the French Resistance launched a massive uprising in Paris. Terribly weakened by the fighting in Normandy, the Germans were unable to create an effective response. Hitler preferred to see the city burn than allow it to be taken from his grasp, and on the 25th Free French and American forces reached Paris to ensure that did not happen. The capital of France had been liberated, a hugely symbolic moment.

The fighting in France wasn't over, but with the fall of the Falaise Pocket, the outcome was decided. The Allies, now under the overall command of Eisenhower rather than Montgomery, began a great push east. Less than a year after those first brave men leapt off the landing craft in Normandy and waded up the surf into the mouths of German guns, the German empire had fallen. Hitler was dead. His nation was conquered. The atrocities of his regime had been exposed, and the perpetrators sat awaiting trial for their crimes. The D-Day landings played a crucial part in making that happen.

More than 70 years on, it's easy to forget what a staggering and unprecedented achievement D-Day was. It took colossal political, strategic, and logistical efforts to bring together the armed forces of so many countries, to create a plan so daring, and to bring together the resources needed to carry it off.

It also took courage. The men who stepped out onto those beaches knew they were likely walking into a bloodbath. They had trained and prepared for this moment, but it was no less incredible they were willing to put their lives on the line and that, even in the toughest sectors, they made it work. They did not achieve all their objectives because those objectives were ambitious, not because they faltered or failed. Their actions shaped the face of Europe and left an unprecedented mark in the annals of history.

Long may their memory live on.

Can you help me?

If you enjoyed this book, then I'd really appreciate it if you would post a short review on Amazon. I read all the reviews myself so that I can continue to provide books that people want.

Thanks for your support!

Preview of World War 2
A Captivating Guide from Beginning to End

Introduction

The Second World War was one of the most traumatic events in human history. Across the world, existing conflicts became connected, entangling nations in a vast web of violence. It was fought on land, sea, and air, touching every inhabited continent. Over 55 million people died, some of them combatants, some civilians caught up in the violence, and some murdered by their own governments.

It was the war that unleashed the Holocaust and the atomic bomb upon the world. But it was also a war that featured acts of courage and self-sacrifice on every side.

The world would never be the same again.

Chapter 1 – The Rising Tide

The Second World War grew out of conflicts in two parts of the world: Europe and East Asia. Though the two would eventually become entangled, it's easier to understand the causes of the war by looking at them separately.

Europe's problems were rooted in centuries of competition between powerful nations crammed together on a small and densely populated continent. Most of the world's toughest, most stubborn, and most ambitious kids were crammed together in a single small playground. Conflict was all but inevitable.

The most recent large European conflict had been the First World War. This was the first industrialized war, a hugely traumatic event for all the participants. In the aftermath, Germany was severely punished for its aggression by the victorious Allied powers. The remains of the Austro-Hungarian empire fell apart, creating instability in the east. And the Russian Empire, whose government had been overthrown during the turmoil of the war, became the Union of Soviet Socialist Republics (USSR), the first global power to adopt the new ideology of communism.

From this situation of instability, a new form of politics emerged. Across Europe, extreme right-wing parties adopted ultra-nationalistic views. Many of them incorporated ideas of racial superiority. Most were strongly influenced by the fear of communism. All relied on scapegoating outsiders to make themselves more powerful.

The first to reach prominence was the Fascist Party in Italy under Benito Mussolini. Mussolini was a veteran soldier, gifted orator, and skilled administrator. He rallied disenchanted left-wingers and those who felt put down by corrupt politicians and forceful trade unions. Using a mixture of persuasion and intimidation, he won the 1922 election and became prime minister. Through a series of laws, he turned his country into a one-party dictatorship. Most of his achievements were domestic, bringing order and efficiency at the price of freedom, but he also had ambitions abroad. He wanted Italy to be a colonial power like Britain or France, and so in 1935-6 his forces conquered Abyssinia.

Mussolini was surpassed in almost every way by the man who reached power in Germany a decade later—Adolph Hitler. A decorated veteran of the First World War, Hitler was embittered at the Versailles Treaty, which imposed crushing restrictions upon Germany in the aftermath of the war. He developed a monstrous ideology that combined racism, homophobia, and a bitter hatred of communism. Like Mussolini, he brought together oratory and street violence to seize control of Germany. Once elected chancellor in 1933, he purged all opposition and had himself made Führer, the nation's "leader" or "guide." He then escalated the rearmament of

Germany, casting off the shackles of Versailles.

Hitler and Mussolini intervened in the Spanish Civil War of 1936-9. Rather than have their nations join the war, they sent parts of their armed forces to support Franco's right-wing armies, testing new military technology and tactics while ensuring the victory of a man they expected to be an ally—a man who would in fact keep his nation out of the coming war for Europe.

Meanwhile, Hitler was playing a game of chicken with the other European powers. In March 1936, he occupied the Rhineland, a part of Germany that had been demilitarized after the war. Two years later, he annexed his own homeland of Austria, with its large German-speaking population. He occupied parts of Czechoslovakia that fall and finished the job off the following spring. At every turn, the rest of Europe backed down rather than go to war to protect less powerful nations.

Meanwhile, in Asia, the Chinese revolutions of 1911 and 1913, along with the Chinese Civil War that broke out in 1927, had triggered a parallel period of instability. Nationalists and communists battled for control of a vast nation, destroying the regional balance of power.

Japan was a nation on the rise. Economic growth had created a sense of ambition which had then been threatened by a downturn in the 1930s. Interventions by Western powers, including their colonies in Asia and a restrictive naval treaty of 1930, embittered many in Japan, who saw the Europeans and Americans as colonialist outsiders meddling in their part of the world.

The Japanese began a period of expansion, looking to increase their political dominance and their control of valuable raw resources. They invaded Chinese Manchuria in 1931 and from then on kept encroaching on Chinese territory. At last, in 1937, the Chinese nationalist leader Chiang Kai-Shek gave up on his previous policy of giving ground to buy himself time. A minor skirmish escalated into the Second Sino-Japanese War.

From an Asian point of view, the war had already begun. But it would be Hitler who pushed Europe over the brink and gave the war its Western start date of 1939.

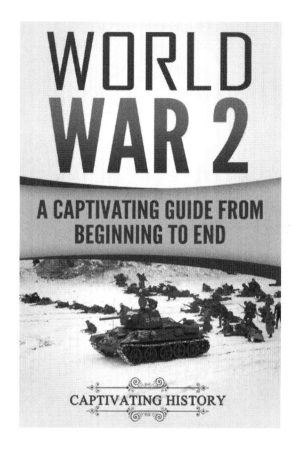

Check out this book!

Preview of Korean War
A Captivating Guide to Korean War History

Introduction

The narrative of the Korean War in the West, and particularly in the United States, tells the tale of a conflict between two global superpowers and competing ideologies in a far-flung corner of the globe.

The reality is that the wheels of motion that drove the country to war in 1950 began turning long before American boots set foot on Korean soil. The heart of the conflict was a civil war between a population arbitrarily divided by colonization and the global geopolitics at the end of the Second World War.

Challenging the widely perpetuated Western narrative and getting to the core of the Korean conflict is no easy feat. From assumptions that the outbreak of war was a deliberate act of communist aggression, to the notion that Eisenhower and Truman's constant threats of atomic annihilation broke the Chinese and North Korean spirit and led to the signing of the armistice, everything needs to be dissected and reviewed on its own factual merit to fully understand the nature of the war.

This guide seeks to pull this narrative curtain and peek behind at the truth of the matter, tracing the history of the war back to the Japanese occupation and uncovering the root of Korean nationalism that stirred the nation into the frenzy of civil war in 1950.

It is about an often-forgotten war, fighting for its place in history between the two behemoths of the Second World War and the Vietnam War, which was no less significant, no less destructive, and had no less impact on the global politics of the twentieth century.

Four Maps of the Korean War

June 25, 1950 | Sept. 14, 1950 | Nov. 25, 1950 | July 27, 1953

Chapter 1 – The Japanese Ascendency: 1910-1945

The chain of events that brought the Korean peninsula to the outbreak of war in 1950 can be traced back to almost half a century before, at the beginning of the Japanese occupation of the country. The Korean nation, with a shared culture, language, ethnicity and heritage, deteriorated from harmonious social cohesion to a bloody civil war in just 40 years. The scars of the conflict are still etched on the Korean political landscape today. The North has a reclusive communist government, while the South has flourished as a democratic republic.

To understand the rapid deterioration and ultimate segregation of the peninsula, we must examine the conditions of the Japanese occupation of the country. Koreans under Japanese rule were a systematically divided and oppressed population. They saw their culture suppressed and their workforce mobilized to feed Japanese mouths and drive the Japanese war machine. But the period also gave birth to the Korean independence movement and began to shape Korean nationalism. Nationalist ideas would begin to be formed, both within Korea itself, across the Yalu River in China, and within the Soviet Union by those in exile. These same ideas which were bred under Japanese rule are those that gave the peninsula the political divide we can still see today.

The Japan-Korea Annexation Treaty of 1910

After formally becoming a Japanese protectorate in 1905 and handing over control of administrative affairs to the Japanese in 1907, Japanese Resident General Count Terauchi Masatake drew up the Japan-Korea Annexation Treaty in 1910, to formally transfer the governance of Korea to the Emperor of Japan. When presented with the treaty, Emperor Sunjong of Korea had no intention of signing it. But, with the ominous threat of Japanese invasion looming if he didn't, he reluctantly placed his national seal of the Korean Empire on the treaty and, rather than sign it himself, presented Prime Minister Lee Wan-yong with the document to signi.

Sunjong faced the dilemma of either signing the document and accepting Japanese rule, or resist and be taken by force, which would undoubtedly have left many casualties and led to a more submissive relationship under the Japanese government. The fact the Emperor himself didn't actually sign the document, and the conditions of duress that the document was presented under, has led many subsequent governments of both South and North Korea to question the legality of the treaty.

Life under Japanese rule

Despite the Emperor's seal, the Koreans were treated as conquered people. The Japanese implemented their version of military rule, known as budan seijiii. The military and police extended their control into every aspect of Korean life. Koreans were not allowed to publish their own newspapers or organize their own political groupsiii, nor were they included in high levels of government administration. Korean land was frequently confiscated by the Japanese and redistributed.

Economically, the Japanese implemented a system of protectionist capitalism. They used Korean labor to drive Japanese industries. Koreans found themselves working in Japanese-owned firms. Any profits were sent back to Japaniv and only a very small and select group of Korean elites became successful under Japanese rule. In 1942, Korean entrepreneurs owned just 1.5% of the total capital invested in Korean industries and they were charged interest rates up to 25% higher than their Japanese counterpartsv. These conditions made it impossible for the Korean working class to improve their lot and eroded the wealth of the already established middle class.

The Japanese occupiers wanted to ensure total stability and control on the peninsula, which would provide a buffer area between them and Chinese aggressionvi. Their intention was to use the Korean peninsula to expand into northeast China and take the Chinese region of Manchuria.

They used Korea to fill a grain shortage in Japan. Rice and soybeans were exported from Korea to Osaka, Yokohama, and Yagasakivii. As more and more grain left the country to feed the Japanese occupiers, there was less to go around for the Korean population. Between 1932 and 1936, the rice consumption per capita in Korea was half of what it had been from 1912 to 1916viii.

The March First Movement

But the Koreans, who had been used to self-rule within the Chinese Orbit and were proud of their cultural traditions, were a cohesive social society. A resistance movement had been forming throughout the first decade of

Japanese rule and on 1 March, 1919, 33 activists publicly read a Korean Declaration of Independence in Seoul and aired their complaints on the radio and in the newspapers.

Public protests spread across the country that day and Japanese forces responded with bloodshed and violence. Korean sources claim 7,509 people were killed by Japanese military forces, while Japanese officials are adamant the figure is lower, at 553 people. The protests were suppressed through the military, but the Korean population had made a prominent statement.

The second phase of the Japanese Occupation

In the wake of the demonstrations, the Japanese occupation under Admiral Saito Makoto entered a new phase. Unlike the iron-fisted military rule of his predecessor, Makoto ushered in a period of cultural rule (bunka seiji)ix. The strict controls on Korean culture were eased, Koreans could publish their own newspapers and laws against public expression and gathering were lifted.

But the changes were short lived. In the 1930s, the military took control of the Japanese government and the Korean colony was required to play a more important role in forging a Japanese Empire. The Japanese launched their campaign into China in 1931, taking Manchuria and creating the Japanese state of Manchukuo. It was at this point the Japanese adopted a policy of assimilation towards the Korean population. Worship at Shinto Shrines became mandatoryx and Korean families were forced to take Japanese family names. Korean schools were forbidden from using the Korean language and all education was given in Japanese.

In 1937, Japan embarked on the second Sino-Japanese War against China. The whole of the Japanese Empire was placed on war footing, including the Korean population. The Korean economy was modified to support the war effort. Heavy industries were introduced, with the construction of large scale chemical and electrical plantsxi. The transportation systems were modified to cater for the distribution of resources and troops to Manchukuo, to the north of the peninsula. Although the profits were still being funneled back to Japan, the Sino-Japanese war was a period of intense economic development. They created Korean industries and brought the country away from merely agricultural development, which brought many benefits to the country in the years following the occupation.

The Japanese continued their efforts to strip the Korean population of any semblance of a national identity and culture and impose their own on the peninsula. By 1940, 84% of all Korean families had adopted Japanese names, only the Japanese language was spoken in schools and in public spheres, and they had shut down all Korean newspapers and media publications after the outbreak of warxii. But, in doing so, the Japanese had instigated a prominent Korean nationalist movement.

The Birth of Korean Nationalism

The Japanese occupation of the Korean peninsula created the perfect conditions for a resistance movement to grow. The yangban (landowning class) and the urban middle class, resented the Japanese occupation and the lack of opportunities it offered. While a select few Korean elites were becoming wealthy through collaboration with the Japanese occupiers, the majority were made landless and reduced to a state of poverty by Japanese rulexiii.

During the first phase of the occupation, the nationalist movement was focused on middle-class yangban students. They regularly organized protests and engaged in pro-independence activities. The movement received financial backing from some political elites of the country, like Kim Song-su, a wealthy Korean entrepreneur who made his fortunes in the textile industry. But these entrepreneurs had to be careful. They were in business with the Japanese regime and any support for independence movements was risky and needed to be discretexiv.

In the early occupation period, nationalist movements among the poorer rural classes manifested themselves as small flare-ups of insurrections. Calling themselves the Righteous Army, their rebellions were disorganized and were easily put down by the Japanese military throughout the 1910s and 1920s. For the rural classes, these small revolts were driven more by anger over poverty and inequality than actual nationalist ideology.

Many Korean intellectuals and nationalists were living in exile in Soviet Russia and China, after fleeing Korea during its annexation. After the October Revolution in 1917 and the perpetuation of communist ideas across Asia, the appetite to form a pro-independence, communist movement in Korea grew. In 1918, in Irkutsk, Soviet Russia, the First Korean Communist Party was formed by Koreans living in exilexv. Although considered part of the Russian Communist Party, it was organized as the Korean Section.

In Shanghai, the center of the Chinese working class movement, Koreans living in exile formed a Provisional Government of Korea. They also embraced socialism as a solution to Korea's problems. The Provincial Government declared a ruling coalition with the newly formed Koryo Communist Partyxvi, led by Yi Tong-hwi, a former Korean army officer. Yi Tong-hwi and his counterparts in Russia used their ties and connections to spread their socialist agenda within the Korean peninsula.

Their effort was rewarded in 1925 when the Korean Communist Party was formed, on Korean soilxvii. However, maintaining a national communist party in Korea was a risky business. Their charismatic leader, Pak Hon-yong, had been in the Shanghai faction in 1921 and returned to Korea to form the Korean Communist Party, aged just 25. He was imprisoned first by the Japanese Military in 1925, shortly after the formation of the party, and spent four years in prison. In 1933, he was arrested again. This time, the Japanese systematically tortured him and kept him in isolation for the next six years, to the point that they believed him to be insane and incapable of leading a movement when they released him in 1939. But he came out and reformed the party, eventually fleeing to South Cholla to avoid re-arrestxviii.

The Provisional Government in Shanghai were also busy making preparations to re-enter Korea. Kim Ku, a prominent figure in the Provisional Government, organized high-profile assassinations of Japanese high officials. He also met with Chinese leader Chiang Kai-shek in 1933 to secure financial aid for the nationalist cause. Ku promised that in return for financial support from the Chinese Government, the Provisional Government in exile would generate uprisings against the Japanese in Japan, Korea, and Manchuria (Manchukuo) within the next two yearsxix. While Chiang Kai-shek refused to give the desired financial support, he did begin a scheme whereby the Chinese forces would train military cadets for the Korean Provisional Governmentxx. However, the scheme was abandoned a year later, after heavy protest from Japan.

In the later part of the occupation, when the Japanese embarked on their aggressive assimilation policy, the Korean nationalist movement was forced into exile once again. It became too dangerous to remain in Korea and continue operations and surviving leaders of the movements described a time of constant police surveillance and job discrimination wherever they turnedxxi. Many went across the border into China and joined the Provisional Government in Shanghai. Some fled across the Yalu River into Japan's newly created state of Manchukuo and embarked on guerrilla operations to undermine the Japanese occupation there. Their goal was to form a people's army in Manchukuo which, with the support of Mao Zedong and the other Chinese Communists, would reenter Korea and overthrow the Japanese government.

The period under the Japanese ascendancy shows a population with a strongly nationalist consciousness, but the extensive repressive measures in place prevented a single nationalist leader rising to the forefront of a Korean movement. There were several movements operating from abroad, and within the country, the student movement, the exiles in Soviet Russia, the exiles in China, the Righteous Army, the peasant movement, and the guerilla operations in Manchuria, but there was no single banner to unite and rally a population. As a result, the movement's effectiveness was severely limited under the Japanese occupation.

World War II

When World War II began in the Pacific in 1941, the Korean population was once again placed on war footing to support the Japanese effort. Half a million Koreans were forced into serving in the Japanese army. They did not receive equal treatment to the Japanese soldiers. The Japanese put their Korean soldiers in higher risk situations because they saw them as more expendable than their Japanese counterpartsxxii.

If war was tough on the Korean male population, it was outright torture for the female population. Some 200,000xxiii Korean women were forced into military brothels. Known as 'comfort women', these women were subjected to beatings, torture, and rape, and kept in conditions no better than most slaughterhousesxxiv. Many of the women never returned to their homes after the war. Many died during their ordeal, others died later due to the physical and psychological trauma they suffered, but also some refused to go home due to the intense feeling of shame. Today the Japanese government still refuse to acknowledge these 'comfort women' existed, despite the numerous accounts from survivorsxxv.

The Japanese Legacy

On 15 August 1945, the war ended. Japan surrendered to Allied forces and their 35-year occupation of the Korean peninsula came to an end. The Japanese left a divided Korean population with almost no middle class. A few Korean families who had collaborated with the Japanese had amassed a huge amount of wealth under the period of economic development, but the majority of the Korean population was left impoverished and without land. The blatant inequality between those who had collaborated with the Japanese and those who hadn't, left a population acutely sensitive to the injustices created under Japanese capitalism. In the wake of World War

II, they hoped for an independent government which could address the issues of inequality and poverty.

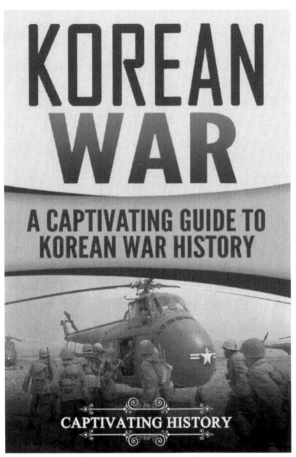

Check out this book!

Free Bonus from Captivating History (Available for a Limited time)

Hi History Lovers!

Now you have a chance to join our exclusive history list so you can get your first history ebook for free as well as discounts and a potential to get more history books for free! Simply visit the link below to join.

Captivatinghistory.com/ebook

Also, make sure to follow us on:

Twitter: @Captivhistory

Facebook: Captivating History: @captivatinghistory

Bibliography

Ralph Bennett (1999), Behind the Battle: Intelligence in the War with Germany 1939-1945.

Gordon Brown (2008), Wartime Courage.

Nigel Cawthorne (2004), Turning the Tide: Decisive Battles of the Second World War.

David Chandler and Ian Beckett (eds) (1994), The Oxford History of the British Army.

Christopher Chant (1986), The New Encyclopedia of Handguns.

Francis Crosby (2010), The Complete Guide to Fighters & Bombers of the World.

Ian Dear (1997), Escape and Evasion: POW Breakouts in World War Two.

John Ellis (1993), The World War II Databook.

Max Hastings (1984), Overlord: D-Day and the Battle for Normandy 1944.

Ian V. Hogg and John Weeks (1980), The Illustrated Encyclopedia of Military Vehicles.

Richard Holmes, ed. (2001), The Oxford Companion to Military History.

James Lucas (1996), Hitler's Enforcers: Leaders of the German War Machine 1939-1945.

Russell Miller (2002), Behind the Lines: The Oral History of Special Operations in World War II.

David Rooney (1999), Military Mavericks: Extraordinary Men of Battle.

Korean War:

---

[i] Kawasaki, Yutaka. "Was the 1910 Annexation Treaty Between Korea and Japan Concluded Illegally", *Murdoch University Electronic Journal of Law*, 3,2 (1996). http://www.murdoch.edu.au/elaw/issues/v3n2/kawasaki.html. [Accessed 1 Aug 2017]

[ii] McNamara, Dennis L. *The Colonial Origins of Korean Enterprise: 1910-1945* (Cambridge: Cambridge University Press: 1990) p.36

[iii] Savada, Andrea Matles and Shaw, William. Eds. *South Korea: A Country Study* (Washington: GPO for the Library of Congress: 1990) http://countrystudies.us/south-korea/7.htm Accessed: [1 Aug 2017]

[iv] McNamara, Dennis L. *The Colonial Origins of Korean Enterprise: 1910-1945* (Cambridge: Cambridge University Press: 1990) p.36

[v] Savada, Andrea Matles and Shaw, William. Eds. *South Korea: A Country Study* (Washington: GPO for the Library of Congress: 1990) http://countrystudies.us/south-korea/7.htm Accessed: [1 Aug 2017]

[vi] McNamara, Dennis L. *The Colonial Origins of Korean Enterprise: 1910-1945* (Cambridge: Cambridge University Press: 1990) p.34

[vii] McNamara, Dennis L. *The Colonial Origins of Korean Enterprise: 1910-1945* (Cambridge: Cambridge University Press: 1990) p.36

[viii] Savada, Andrea Matles and Shaw, William. Eds. *South Korea: A Country Study* (Washington: GPO for the Library of Congress: 1990) http://countrystudies.us/south-korea/7.htm Accessed: [1 Aug 2017]

[ix] McNamara, Dennis L. *The Colonial Origins of Korean Enterprise: 1910-1945* (Cambridge: Cambridge University Press: 1990) p.36

[x] Savada, Andrea Matles and Shaw, William. Eds. *South Korea: A Country Study* (Washington: GPO for the Library of Congress: 1990) http://countrystudies.us/south-korea/7.htm [Accessed: 1 Aug 2017]

[xi] McNamara, Dennis L. *The Colonial Origins of Korean Enterprise: 1910-1945* (Cambridge: Cambridge University Press: 1990) p.36

[xii] Savada, Andrea Matles and Shaw, William. Eds. *South Korea: A Country Study* (Washington: GPO for the Library of Congress: 1990) http://countrystudies.us/south-korea/7.htm [Accessed: 1 Aug 2017]

[xiii] Pang, Kie-chung, *Landlords, Peasants and Intellectuals in Modern Korea* (Ithaka, NY: Cornell University: 2005)

[xiv] Millet, Alan R. "The Korean People Missing in Action in the Misunderstood War, 1845-1954" in Stueck, Wiliam, ed. *The Korean War in World History* (Kentucky: University Press of Kentucky: 2004) p.13

[xv] Ibid. P.17

[xvi] Ibid.

[xvii] Ibid. P.18

[xviii] Ibid

[xix] Liu, Xiaoyuan, "Sino-American Diplomacy over Korea During World War II" in *The Journal of American-East Asian Relations*, 1, 2 (1992) p.233

[xx] Ibid

[xxi] Millet, Alan R. "The Korean People Missing in Action in the Misunderstood War, 1845-1954" in Stueck, Wiliam, ed. *The Korean War in World History* (Kentucky: University Press of Kentucky: 2004) p.17

[xxii] Daws, Gavan, *Prisoners of the Japanese: POWs of World War II in the Pacific* (New York: W. Morrow: 1994)

[xxiii] Shoten, Iwanami, *Comfort Women: Sexual Slavery in Japanese Military During World War II*, (New York: Columbia University Press: 2000)

[xxiv] Williamson, Lucy, 'Comfort Women: South Korea's Survivors of Japanese Brothels', *BBC News*, 2013, http://www.bbc.com/news/magazine-22680705, [Accessed 3 Aug, 2017]

[xxv] Ibid.

ABOUT CAPTIVATING HISTORY

A lot of history books just contain dry facts that will eventually bore the reader. That's why Captivating History was created. Now you can enjoy history books that will mesmerize you. But be careful though, hours can fly by, and before you know it; you're up reading way past bedtime.

Get your first history book for free here:
http://www.captivatinghistory.com/ebook

Make sure to follow us on Twitter:

@CaptivHistory
and Facebook:
www.facebook.com/captivatinghistory so you
can get all of our updates!

Made in the USA
San Bernardino,
CA

58853503R00104